12 Keys to Success for Misfits, Weirdos & Introverts:

A Practical and Spiritual Guide to
Understanding Your Place in the World

By: Tiffany Jackson

Deep Roots Publishing

info@deeprootspublishing.com

This book is dedicated to every kind soul that has helped me in this journey called life. It is dedicated to those who have embraced me while I searched for my place in this world. Though very imperfect, you saw fit to love me anyway. Most importantly, thank you God for all you have done for me. There are no words that could ever express how grateful I am for how much you have kept me, loved me, guided me, and blessed me. I will always be your willing, obedient, and thankful servant.

TABLE OF CONTENTS

INTRODUCTION

Before you take your first step on this journey, I must advise you that if you bought this book to help you climb the corporate ladder or learn how to be a better networker, leader, or salesperson, please note that this is not that kind of self-help book. However, if you want to understand how to manage your uniqueness in a world of conformity, then please continue to read.

You must understand that success is more than just the accumulation of money and material things; it is understanding yourself and your role in the world so that you can fulfill your ultimate purpose. It is learning how to leverage your gifts and master the traits and characteristics that make you different. I sincerely believe that everyone can experience real success, both in tangible and intangible ways, but I do not believe that the same set of steps will get everyone to that place.

Oftentimes, mainstream advice does not apply to individuals who do not fit within the norm. Conventional advice appears to be impossible for unique individuals to follow. This is because they don't have the social acceptance necessary to fulfill the steps that have been outlined as mandatory for success. What I have discovered is that obtaining success as an outsider is far more about how you think than following a specific rule set. I say this because your actions will always follow your thoughts. This is not to diminish the importance of action, but rather to say your thoughts will guide your actions, and consequently, your thought life has to be ordered for the path that you are on. The rules are different for outsiders. Therefore, your approach should different be as well.

This is where this journey begins—understanding how to approach your life and career in a way where your differences are not handicaps, but rather real advantages. At a bare minimum, you don't want them to be a barrier that keeps you from achieving the goals you have set for yourself. This journey of self-discovery will not be easy; it will require you to be very honest about where you are, how you think, what you want, and how you feel. Nevertheless, the internal work you do today will pay off in dividends in the future. Why? Because you have to understand yourself and prepare yourself properly to achieve the success that was meant for your life.

I believe the fact that you were drawn to this book speaks volumes about where you are in your journey, as well as your state of readiness for change and success. I do not believe there are coincidences, and it is by divine appointment that you are holding this book. There is a Chinese proverb that states, "When the student is ready, the teacher will appear."

The most fundamental truth about being a misfit is that you are not supposed to change yourself to be successful, but rather, you must change the way you think. Let that sink in. You probably have spent years trying to be something that you are not, and you have never been able to achieve that goal. That is because your success will not come from being like everyone one else. Your success will come when you embrace who you are, and when you become your best and truest self.

Perhaps you are wondering why I included introverts in with

misfits and weirdos. Most people think that introverts are just shy in nature, but what makes introverts different is how they process their thoughts and emotions. We live in an age where connectedness is more important than ever. Networks and circles can make or break a career, however, introverts struggle with the constant pressure to connect, work in teams, and build relationships with others. That is because introverts tend to feel drained after extended interactions with others, and because they need time alone to process information more effectively. Managing introversion in a world that demands extroverted behavior for success is difficult. Therefore, this unique challenge is just as daunting as being the more recognizable misfit or weirdo.

In this book, there are twelve basic principles that misfits, weirdos, and introverts should follow to address their unique challenges in the workplace and life. Each chapter will also include personal life stories from myself and others that show how these basic principles help misfits to succeed. This book is meant to challenge and change the very core assumptions you have about yourself and life. These are not twelve steps to success, but rather twelve new ways of how to approach life.

So many times we live with many false beliefs about ourselves and life that we don't even know we have. For example, most people consciously or unconsciously believe that those who work the hardest are those who succeed. That is not true. Yet day in and day out, millions of people work really hard, thinking that is all they need to be successful. We've also been given advice that not only doesn't apply to misfits, but that can sometimes be harmful to us. I will show in this book why those approaches will not work for you.

This book is about helping you break out of the useless mindsets that are only holding you back. You can't rely on conventional wisdom to get ahead when you are an unconventional person. Accordingly, the first step to experiencing success as a misfit is to determine if you are one. Please answer the questions below to find out.

How to Tell If You Are a Misfit, Weirdo, or Introvert

1. Do you feel cursed or unlucky?

2. Do you experience social anxiety?

3. Do you feel like people don't like you the moment they meet you?

4. Do you frequently suffer from foot-in-mouth syndrome?

5. Can you count your friends on one hand?

6. Do you feel like it's impossible to meet your goals because of your inability to relate to other people?

7. Do you feel overwhelmed by the number of your dreams and goals you have?

If you answered yes to most of these questions, then that is a good sign you are a misfit, weirdo, or introvert. And if you're ready to change your outlook and your life, then keep reading!

CHAPTER 1

Being "Nice" Isn't Enough

"The person who follows the crowd will usually go no further than the crowd. The person who walks alone is likely to find himself in places no one has ever seen before."

—Albert Einstein

Oftentimes when we don't fit in with society and our present surroundings, the first thing we think is, "What is wrong with me?" These thoughts become especially pervasive if we continue to be misfits even with a change of situation, scenarios, and people. No one wants to stand out, be different, or worse—ostracized. But that comes with the territory when you are a misfit, a weirdo, or an introvert. Unfortunately, as a misfit, you will face rejection regardless of what you do. That doesn't mean you can't experience success or happiness; it just means that how you attain it will be different.

One of the most common assumptions misfits make is to think that being "nice" is enough to make up for the characteristics that make you different. However, being nice will not get you inducted into a social circle or accepted by others. Many misfits believe that if they are "nice," they won't stand out, be called out, or left out. That simply isn't true. Their hope is to go unnoticed, and to have whatever strangeness there is about them canceled out by a gentle, and sometimes passive, nature. Is this to say that you shouldn't be a nice person? Absolutely not! What I am saying is that misfits use this as a tool to overcome being different, but it is simply an ineffective one.

As a misfit, you just can't play by the rules because the rules are different for you. What others do to get ahead will not work for you. At a minimum, you will have to do those things in addition to something else just to get the same results. Others might naturally win the affection and respect of others, but that is not the case for you. You are a person who is intrinsically unique, and to be successful, you constantly have to think on your feet to see how *you* can have success in a specific situation.

I hope what I am about to say is not misconstrued, but the truth of the matter is being a misfit is sort of like having a physical disability. When someone who is in a wheelchair goes out, they have to think about more things than an able-bodied person. They have to figure out if there are ramps for the buildings with stairs, if doors and walkways will be wide enough for their wheelchair, or if there be a handicap-friendly restroom. They have to worry about if they will be able to reach objects placed very high, if they will be able to see the main event, and so many more things that able-bodies individuals never think about. Well, in a social way, misfits, weirdos, and introverts have to consider their possible challenges, too.

For example, when you attend something like a networking event, you may find it is much harder for you to make small talk, connect with others, and make great contacts. You have to go into the event with a plan, as well as with resilience and determination for any rejection you might encounter. You have to be more thoughtful and strategic about what you say or do so that you can accomplish your goals. Before you enter the event, you can benefit from preparing a list of proven conversation starters, already knowing who you want to speak to at the event, and from practicing selling yourself or your idea prior to that day. These actions, along with listening more than talking, will increase your chances of success more than just being "nice" will.

The key to being successful as a misfit is going into to any situation mentally and emotionally prepared. You have to know your weaknesses and strengths as well as how you will manage each, respectively. Your actions will have to be much more deliberate than someone who is naturally outgoing and charismatic. Whenever I go someplace, I am highly conscious of how I am so that I can proactively manage my weaknesses while consciously utilizing my strengths.

Another critical mistake misfits make in their professional lives is to focus on perception versus reality. The heart of success will always be your performance. Even though it is not the only factor, it is the foundation. Your first focus in your career should be the three P's: being punctual, professional, and productive. If you haven't mastered all three areas, the last thing you should be worried about is if others like you. Success for anyone will start with how well they complete the tasks they are given. Therefore, master the three Ps before tackling the specific issues associated with being different from those around you.

I have found that being excellent or the best in my area is highly effective to overcoming the social challenges misfits face. Perceptions of you can and will change once people see you as a leader or expert in your field. Your knowledge and abilities will become much more important to others when you demonstrate a high degree of competence. Most rewarding is that fact that when you perform at a high level, you won't have to go to people, but instead they will come to you. People are drawn toward excellence. Just look at our sports stars! People buy the jerseys of the best players, not the worst.

Becoming a leader in your field will also help you to miss some of the common workplace pitfalls that others fall into. When you are concentrating on being excellent, your time and energy are not focused on unproductive activities. You would be surprised at how many people come to work to do everything except work. Many come to gossip, play on social media, complete schoolwork, flirt with the opposite sex, stir up trouble for their amusement, or just to look and feel important. Some are even so entangled in interoffice politics that they can scarcely focus on anything else. Try to stay out of gossip that is thinly disguised as camaraderie. Remember, if they speak ill of others to you, they will speak ill of you to others.

It is easy to become upset when you see people getting ahead by backstabbing, politicking, and butt-kissing, but reserve your energy for what you need to do to achieve your goals. Psalms 37:1-2 says, "Do not fret because of those who are evil or be envious of those who do wrong; for like the grass they will soon wither, like green plants they will soon die away." In many organizations, there are plenty of busybodies, but very few dedicated workers. The great news is that this presents an opportunity for you to shine based on your work performance alone. One of my favorite song lyrics goes, "It's crowded at the bottom, but there's room at the top," and I have found this to be very true.

Another important lesson I learned about putting work first came from a roommate I had. I had a Jamaican roommate who always quoted her mother as saying, "Yuh come fi drink milk an' nuh fi count cow." This translates to, "you are here to drink milk, and not to count cows." Her mother made it clear to her not to focus on what others had or were doing, but to focus on getting what she needed. Focusing on others puts you in a "how come?" mentality. Instead of working towards your own goals, you get caught up in the mindset of *how come he gets to do this*, or *how come she gets away with that?* What others have doesn't add money to your pocket. What they get to do doesn't affect whether you accomplish your goals. So when you go to work, remember to the drink milk and not to count cows.

It can also be easy for people to fall into the trap of wasting their precious time and energy trying to be liked, thinking it will help them become successful. This is a critical error. Remember, your success does not hinge on whether or not everyone likes you. Would it be nice? Yes. But let me be very clear: *it is not a necessity.* Success affects the number of friends you have infinitely more than how the number of friends you have affects your success. Yes, networks can be very important to help you move ahead, especially in certain industries, but just know that they can only enhance your success, not prevent it. This false belief about needing the approval of others has created an atmosphere where many people are manically trying to join whatever club, network, or group they can because they think they need the validation of the crowd to move ahead. They don't realize that they determine their own success—it is not determined by others.

For ten years, Winston Churchill was at odds with his political party over differences in ideology. Yet that did not stop him from becoming the Prime Minister of the United Kingdom, not to mention one of the greatest war leaders in history. Likewise, even if I become friends with Oprah, that doesn't mean I will be successful. Just being her friend will not make me a billionaire. My success will ultimately be determined by what I do.

Instead of focusing on trying to make everyone like you, work as if you work for yourself. Set your own standards and answer to yourself. Ask yourself this question: "If I were the boss, would I be happy with my current work performance?"

When you go to work, create a positive atmosphere for yourself. Post positive quotes or listen to your favorite songs. Don't allow others to change the atmosphere. Let your light outshine any darkness that tries to encroach upon it. If others respond to your light with negativity, find others with positive attitudes to reenergize and lighten the atmosphere. Be sure to meditate on positive thoughts at work so that you are always acting from a place of optimism. When dealing with negative individuals who try to trip you up, just remember the famous words of Mahatma Gandhi: "First they ignore you, then they laugh at you, then they fight you, then you win."

Still, a less understood—and often unspoken—reason why being "nice" doesn't help is because in some cases kindness can be used as a plea for acceptance. If you find your kindness isn't often reciprocated, it could be because it is not coming off as genuine. What you may view as you being "nice" may come off as kissing up. It may reek of desperation, and that will turn a lot of people off. Additionally, some may find a very chipper personality to be annoying and fake. No one is happy and kind all the time, therefore people may feel like they don't know the real you. The hard truth is that if you don't like yourself, you can't expect others to like you, no matter how "nice" you are.

The reverse is true as well. If someone doesn't like or accept themselves, it will be hard for them to accept you and your kindness. Consequently, a rejection of your kindness may not have anything to do with you at all. In the end, your acts of kindness should never be tied to a specific outcome or reaction you want to get from others. Just let it be a genuine reflection of you and what's in your heart.

Kindness should never be used as a means to gain social acceptance, or as a means to win the approval of others. Kindness will not shelter you from rejection, nor is it guaranteed to win you friends. Kindness certainly won't hide your uniqueness or make people think you are just like them. Accordingly, the first thing you have to accept on your journey to success as a misfit is that you are different.

You will be different, act differently, and be treated differently from those around you. You have to accept this fact so that you don't waste your time trying to fit in by being "nice." Your path will not look the same as others', and what it takes for you to be successful will not be the same either. One part of being different is managing not fitting into mainstream conception of how you should be. The other part is managing rejection. Once you learn how to master those two challenges, the sky is the limit. Remember, if your goal is to be like everyone else, then you are not being true to yourself or the purpose God has placed inside you. No amount of kindness will change that.

Chapter Summary

Sometimes it's easy to fall into the trap of believing that being "nice" is enough to overcome the differences you have with those around you, but it is not. Being "nice" will not make people like you, it will not make you fit in, nor will it exclude you from being misunderstood or ostracized. We wrongly believe that people will treat us the same way we treat them, so we work extra hard to be "nice" to everyone. Unfortunately, this is not the case.

Does this mean you should stop being kind? Of course not! You want to be your best self, even when others aren't. You just have to free yourself from this expectation that your kindness will always be returned. If there are those who do not treat you well, you have to learn how to either remove them from your life or mitigate their effect on you.

Turn your attention to being excellent in your work instead of winning the affections of others. If you are not punctual, professional, and productive, it won't matter if people like you; you can't have success without mastering those three principles. Success will bring friendship, admiration, and respect, but just having friends will never bring you success. Accept your uniqueness and know that you alone are enough. You don't need the validation of others; you just need to know yourself and walk in your purpose.

CHAPTER 2

Acceptance Can't Be Bought in a Store

"He who trims himself to suit everyone will soon whittle himself away."

—Raymond Hull

I learned this expensive lesson my senior year of high school. I went to high school with my sister and my favorite cousin, both of whom enjoyed tremendous popularity. I, on the other hand, was a nice, but timid wallflower. However, I decided that in my senior year I was going to be one of the popular kids, and so in my mind, that meant I needed a wardrobe overhaul. I worked during the summer and gradually built up my new wardrobe piece by piece. After I received my check, I would go to the mall and carefully select each new item. I had everything from accessories to jackets and shoes. I even laid them out meticulously in my bedroom in preparation for the upcoming school year.

When the school year arrived, I was excited to show off all the things I had bought. Each morning, I would dress with the utmost care so that I would look the part of the popular kids. Despite all of the time, expense, and care I took, I noticed that my year was not really different from any other year in high school. I realized that what made the popular kids popular was their charisma, humor, talents, and looks. Those with the money to dress well had what they offered enhanced, but it never served as a substitute for their core traits. That valuable lesson saved me a lot of misused dollars throughout college and the rest of my life. While my classmates in college were going into to debt paying for the trendiest outfits, I already knew that doing that wasn't going to get me the acceptance that I wanted.

Maybe you feel the need to look a certain way because you're trying to emulate the people you want to gain approval from. However, if you have someone in your life that will only interact with you if you wear the latest fashion, a face full of makeup, or a head full of fake hair, then this person will not be able to have a positive and substantive relationship with you anyway. Additionally, surrounding yourself with superficial people is damaging to your spirit. You are training yourself to see only outwardly and never inwardly. If others only hang with you because of what you do for them or buy for them, this same principle applies.

Maybe you are not buying things for other, but rather yourself. Sometimes we spend money on things to relieve stress, for a temporary high, or to have a distraction from our current problems. But using visible items to fulfill invisible needs is a recipe for unhappiness. Everything that is of true value–love, family, peace, health, and contentment—can never be bought. Yet we believe the TV and magazine ads that tell us if we buy this, it will draw the love of our lives. If you drink that, you will be happy. If you own this, you will finally feel like a million bucks. We have been trained as consumers to believe that everything you want in life can be bought. This mentality is great for

Fortune 500 companies, but horrible for the millions of souls who honestly believe that happiness is just a purchase away.

Whenever you feel the need to buy something to please others, you should first figure out what it is you want. Are you buying this item because you want to fit into a circle, gain the attention of the opposite sex, or to make yourself feel more attractive? Once you are aware of the goal behind the purchase, you can then figure out a more direct, not to mention cheaper, way to obtain it. If you want to make yourself more attractive to the opposite sex, you can work on you. You can improve your conversation skills, work on your own self-esteem, and find ways to make others feel special, all without going broke.

Chasing trends, especially material ones, is like being a hamster on a wheel. No matter how much you spend or how much effort you put into getting the latest you-name-it, there will always be another cooler, more expensive you-name-it right after it. That finish line just never comes, and you are constantly exerting your time and energy on the never-ending exercise of keeping up. I bet there are people with platform shoes and bellbottoms in their basements now because at some point they believed they had to have these items to be cool. Looking back, I am sure that more than one person sees how ridiculous they looked for the sake of this pursuit.

Additionally, I believe that relying on things to make you important or popular erodes your sense of value and self-esteem. There will be a point where you go from *wanting* the latest trends to feeling like you *need* to have the latest trends. Too many people base their self-esteem on what they own and not who they are. Unfortunately, these individuals haven't realized that they don't possess the items— but rather, the items are possessing them. How many people do you know who are obsessed with keeping their cars spotless? Do you know people who clean their sneakers more than they do their house, or women who won't leave the house until they have a face full of makeup on first? This vanity keeps many people trapped in a cell of fear and insecurity.

The most dangerous aspect of this mentality is that you will eventually begin to judge people the same way you fear you will be judged. If you are scared that you won't be accepted unless you dress "cute" every day, you will start to look down on people who don't take "pride" in their appearance, and those who don't put any "effort" into their appearance. The victim of this cycle will soon become the perpetrator. This is what makes superficiality so dangerous—it not only affects how you view yourself, but also how you treat others.

What most of us will find once we face our fear of being judged is that the majority of our peers aren't concerned about how we look. Things that you are obsessed about with your personal appearance, most others likely don't even notice. We live in a globalized world where trends, styles, and cultures travel like people do. If you look around you right now, you are probably surrounded by those who look, dress, speak, and act very differently from you. (If you live in a homogenized area, a change of locale might be in your best interest.) Regardless of what others do, what is important is that your style reflects who you really are on the inside.

Realistically speaking, what misfits view as cool, nice, or pretty can oftentimes be different from what others think. Your sense of style may be quite eclectic or unique, and you might hesitate to express that openly. Some ideas might keep you up at night, or tie your stomach in knots during the day because you are so worried about how others might perceive you. But the reality is the vast majority of people will not care at all. From personal experience, I've learned then that unless something directly affects them, people don't care about what decisions you are making about yourself. Thus, if you are hesitant to express yourself in a unique way, please don't let the potential opinions of others (especially strangers) hinder you.

When I was in college, I decided to go natural, meaning I decided I would no longer chemically straighten my hair. I decided the best way achieve this goal was to start over and cut all of my hair off. I was very worried about how people would perceive and treat me. Would boys think I looked too manly? Would girls laugh at my near-bald head? It is hard as a woman because so much of your value in society is based on your appearance. Therefore, having a look that is not accepted by mainstream opinions on beauty can be very daunting and challenging.

Despite my fear, I decided to proceed with the haircut. To make sure I didn't chicken out on the way to the barber, I intentionally cut a huge patch of hair out of the middle of my head. About an hour later, I returned to my dorm room with a very low haircut and proceeded to cry my eyes out. The next day I had to brave the world, hair or no hair. The biggest thing that surprised me about other people's reactions was that there essentially were none. Basically, no one cared. What had seemed like such an earth-shattering decision for me did not even register a blip on the radar of others.

What I have found is that most people will be attracted to your confidence, the manner in which you treat them, and the way you make them feel. If you are funny or can make others blush with playful flirting, those qualities will net you friends more than any piece of clothing ever will. Those who others look up to possess qualities which make them unique. In high school, these attributes may be more tangible, like great looks or athletic ability, but in adult life, it's the internal qualities that make you shine— qualities such as loyalty, intelligence, and thoughtfulness.

What are your unique qualities? What are your superlatives? Focus on developing the qualities that make you special. Take your focus off of the outside and put in on the inside. That's not to say your unique qualities can't be expressed outwardly. The point is to put the focus on who you are on the inside versus what you look like on the outside when you try to connect with others.

Sadly, it is easier to rely on outward appearances to fit in, rather than to expose our real selves to rejection. I believe we are often scarred by the teasing and bullying of our childhood, and we carry those insecurities into adulthood. To this day, if someone stares at me, I automatically look away, because growing up I was not used to getting positive attention. I have to make a conscious effort to remember that all attention is not bad attention. Unfortunately, we spend so much of our youth trying to fit in that it becomes counterintuitive to do anything to stick out as an adult. Social norms are strong, but they should not be a barrier that blocks you from expressing your true self. Eleanor Roosevelt once said, "Remember always that you not only have the right to be an individual, you have an obligation to be one."

Even if someone does not agree with how you express yourself, generally, most people will not openly share their opinion. For those who make it a point to say something, they intentionally do it to make you feel bad. They feel obligated to follow certain rules, and they are angry that you are not doing the same. They have been trapped by ideas of what they believe is acceptable, and what is not. They are so convinced of their beliefs that they feel you should have the same convictions as well. You should not take this personally. They sincerely believe they are right, and that there is only one "way" to be. Depending on your relationship with that person, you can either refuse to engage with them, ask them to respect your right to self-expression, or you can try to help them expand their mind.

Those who question you or try to discourage you will generally be the ones closest to you. However, if they can't accept an authentic expression of your truest self, then that is a good sign that they are closer to you than they should be. When you are on a journey of self-awakening, there will be times where close friends and family will not understand changes in your actions, appearance, and life. You will have to be patient with them as they discover the true you. You will also need patience with yourself as you figure out how you want to express yourself. Be open and honest with those you love so they understand the changes they are experiencing with you.

Vincent van Gogh had a very specific artistic style that was not accepted during his time. In fact, during his lifetime, he sold only one painting out of the approximately 900 paintings he completed. Today, his art is heralded around the world, with the most expensive piece having sold for $82,500,000. Image what the world would be robbed of if he had compromised his style to in order be accepted! Now think about what you are robbing the world of by not being your true self.

Ultimately, you can't expect to be accepted by others until you learn to accept yourself. If you don't feel comfortable in your own skin, you can't expect things or people to change that. Changing what you look like on the outside never changes who you truly are on the inside. Still, I have discovered that the only thing worse than trying to stuff yourself into a predetermined box of what hot, pretty, and cool looks like is wasting money doing it.

Your current financial state is a reflection of your mental state. The Bible says in Matthew 6:21, "For where your treasure is, there your heart will be also." If your money is going to superficial things, your heart is set on things that are not uplifting, enduring—or quite frankly—important. Instead of wasting money on insignificant things, try spending your money on things that matter. The best return on your disposable income will always be on things that improve your intangible assets, like your mind, spirit, and personality. Purchases on items such as education, travel, and acquiring new skills all help to make you a better person. A better use of your income is to spend it on appreciable investments and not depreciable assets. Cars, jewelry, and clothes are all items that lose value over time. Investments such as stock, real estate, and education will increase your earnings and net worth in the long run.

Learn about the stock market, if you don't already. Great wealth has been made there. If you are a novice, books like *The Neatest Little Guide to Stock Market Investing* by Jason Kelly are helpful. If you are bad with money and budgeting, get a handle on it now! It will not matter how much money you make if it slips through your fingers every month. If you feel like you have a shopping addiction, seek help. If you can't afford professional help, most pastors offer counseling for free. You can turn over a new leaf by selling some of your used and unused goods and putting the money towards a real investment. Buy a computer, take a class, buy stock, or start a business. Remember, happiness can be shared, divided, or multiplied, but it can never be bought in stores.

Chapter Summary

With a strong sense of self, you can be buoyed through the storms and waves of life instead of being tossed to and fro and left to drown. We live in a society where trends come just as fast as they go. If you changed your speech, dress, hobbies, and outlook every time a fad came by, you would be the most confused, twisted, and exhausted person around. You can't try to contort yourself to fit into every box that pop culture says is cool because that is a surefire way to end up unhappy.

Despite what television, radio, and the internet lead us to believe, we can never buy acceptance. No pair of shoes or smart phone is ever going to make you be something that you are not. If others are drawn to you for those reasons, then it is likely they have no interest in who you are, only what you have.

Work to both enhance and showcase your best personal qualities. This will do more for gaining real acceptance than any purchase ever could. When you want to buy something, first figure out what it is you really want. What we all truly seek is happiness; it is only our belief in what will produce it that makes us different. When we examine our true goals, we will find that there are easier and much cheaper ways to get what we really want. Invest in areas that are proven to add value to you, not only to your pocketbook, but also to your mind and spirit. It is in these areas that we reap the greatest rewards.

Lastly, despite our fears, most people will not judge us for expressing ourselves in a unique way. This is a byproduct of a society that has trained us to be too self-absorbed to notice anything other than ourselves. Therefore, walk in an authentic expression of yourself. Most importantly, eliminate the influence of those who might try to dim your light.

CHAPTER 3

Enjoy You

"Today you are You, that is truer than true. There is no one alive who is Youer than You"

—Dr. Seuss

To make a successful path for yourself in life, you need to know yourself better than anyone else. It is also imperative that you have a healthy sense of self and that you genuinely like who you are. You should not only know yourself, but also have a highly-developed identity as an individual. You must have your own set of values, ideals, opinions, goals, preferences, and propensities. You have to take time to understand yourself, because if you don't know who you are, how can anyone else understand your uniqueness? This is also important because being sure of who you are and truly loving yourself will be an anchor during the times you face rejection.

The first step to accomplishing any of this is first to accept that you are different. This is a hard first step because so many people don't want to be different. They don't want the loneliness and rejection that comes with being unique. However, at some point, you are going to have to be okay with not being entirely understood. You will have to be okay with others not being able to understand your complexity, or not being recognized for all of your great qualities. Despite the fact that everyone won't love or like you, you must still make a commitment to love yourself unconditionally.

After you have accepted your uniqueness, you have to dissect it. You may know that you are different, but you may not realize why. Perhaps the most surprising realization you may have is that you don't actually know who you are. You may have been trying to play a role for so long that you don't even know who you truly are on the inside. You have to be unwrapped from all the fake layers of yourself that have accumulated over the years. These layers may have been put on to either hide or recreate yourself. However, you can't hide behind a mask of something you are not if you are truly to be successful.

This process of discovery might take some time, but it is well worth it. Take an inventory of the things you enjoy and are attracted to. What reoccurring themes do you see in your life? When and where do you feel the most comfortable? Take time to try different ideas out. Take an art class, pick up a sport, or join a group. Try something you've always been intrigued by and see where it leads you. Be honest about how you feel about those around you. Are you around them because you feel like you have to be? Beyond superficial changes in activities, try to figure out what your passions are. What things inspire you? What can't you live without? What are your hidden dreams?

You might even need to spend more time alone to sort out your feelings and be vulnerable enough to be honest. Take walks alone and get in tune with your own spirit. Build a stronger relationship with

God, for with Him lies all answers as well as unfailing guidance. Listen for His voice to help guide you on your path of self-discovery. Read lots of books to open your mind and help your thought life to operate more positively and productively. Use books to change your assumptions and to break the limits you have placed on yourself. Be sure to include the Bible, because that is God's instruction manual for our lives.

In addition to getting to know yourself, it is important that you do the emotional work to make yourself into the best version of you that you can possibly be. Everyone has something that they are struggling with, and it is important to both acknowledge and actively work toward freedom in those areas.

While working for one specific organization, I had accumulated a lot of leave. Thankfully, I was able to take advantage of that and get two months off at one time. It was during this time that I started a very intentional journey of self-discovery, healing, and understanding. I wanted to understand both myself and my life. I wanted to heal from the past, but most of all, I wanted to change. During that time, I read a lot, and books like *Sacred Pampering Principles* and *All the Joy You Can Stand* by Debrena Jackson Gandy were game-changers for me. These books help me to understand how to treat myself and how to view the world around me in a better way. I also targeted books that helped me deal with my own emotional struggles, such as managing anger and overcoming past emotional wounds. For your journey, your book list should focus on the areas in which you need the most help.

If your current job doesn't give you the freedom to take that much time off, I encourage you to read the book *Six Months Off* by Hope

Dlugozima and James Scott. This book offers very practical and creative ways to take anywhere from a few weeks to a year off so you can have the time you need to focus during your journey of self-discovery. Even if you can't take any time off of work, it is important to take time every day—even if it's twenty minutes—and dedicate it to working on yourself. If possible, either do it early in the morning or late at night, because those are times when things are quiet, and you can have the peace you need to meditate and reflect.

You will need some space where you can breathe and just be. Space where there is no pressure to be anything but yourself. We have to lay down our masks and face what we really are if we are to embrace who we are and become our best selves. Any doctor will tell you not to put a bandage over a burn because the air helps it to heal. Well, our hearts and minds are the same way. We can't cover up our hurts and expect them to heal properly. However, because we are exposing ourselves and are in vulnerable and fragile states, it's important to be in a safe space. For me, this is why it is so vitally important to spend time alone. Even if it is a weekend away, it can make a lifetime of difference.

On my own journey, I have to acknowledge that at some points it was difficult to be alone with my emotions. There were times in my life that I thought if I started to cry, I would never stop. It can be a scary proposition to face troubling memories and crippling fears, but it will all be worth it. This is emotional spring cleaning, and your outlook on life will be so much brighter, clearer, and freer because of it. You have to be in tune with your emotions if you are going to be successful as a misfit. You have to get to a point where you can identify every emotion you are feeling and why. You have to not only know what you are feeling, but eventually embrace it and then control it.

If true healing is to take place, there has to be a mourning process as well. You *have* to allow yourself the opportunity to mourn your pain. You have to mourn loss and unfulfilled dreams. Those tears will work as a healing balm on your wounded heart. They will free you from carrying these emotions around forever. If you don't acknowledge your disappointments, they will continue to linger. One of the most freeing practices I have begun is to allow myself to feel whatever emotion comes. If something upsets me, I not only know I am upset, but I can also say it, and feel it. However, because I am conscious of the emotion, I can also control how it manifests. That means I don't snap at a Starbucks barista if someone else has pissed me off.

Once I acknowledge and feel that emotion, for however long it takes for it to go away naturally, it becomes so much easier to let go of. Not to mention it takes much less time to do so. It's like being very angry and having a big blow up. Even though the situation got out of hand, you still feel better because you let that emotion out. That is why you have to allow yourself to feel, otherwise emotions just build up to a point where you can't control them. David Richo has a book called *How to Be an Adult* which is helpful in learning how to process feelings.

When you acknowledge past hurts however, don't expect them all to go away overnight. Sometimes it takes weeks or months to process specific emotions fully. For instance, I had an ex-boyfriend who I thought I was completely over. However, when I found out he had gotten married, I was flooded with all of these emotions I didn't know I still had. To add insult to injury, he married someone who looked very similar to me. At first, I was angry that he would marry a "bootleg" version of me, but when I was honest with myself, I had to admit that I was hurt because I still cared for him.

As I allowed myself to feel the emotions that were coming, the more I uncovered hidden emotions I didn't know I still had. It was like finding an old storage unit and realizing just how much junk you'd locked away. I had unprocessed feelings of hurt, anger, rejection, humiliation, and most surprising of all, love. It took months for me to get to a place where I could finally come to peace with the situation. During those months, I didn't pretend like I wasn't upset when I was. By being conscious of my feelings, I also relived moments of hurt, anger, rejection, and regret. Yet I let myself feel those emotions in order to process them. I went through that storage unit and took inventory of everything that was there. I cried over the bad memories and laughed over the good ones, but most importantly, I threw away the bad and kept the good. My experience with my ex was not all good, nor was it all bad, and I had to admit that to be able to move on with my life. Now I can truthfully say that I have let go of my past with him.

In addition to needing alone time to process emotions, you also need it to seek direction. This quiet time should also be a time for God to speak to our spirit. Psalms 4:4 says, "Commune with your own heart upon your bed, and be still." Sometimes we constantly pray to God about things, but rarely do we give Him an opportunity to answer. After you pray, just spend a couple of minutes meditating on the goodness of the Lord. Give Him an opportunity to speak to your mind and your spirit. In the still moments of the night, God can speak to us about what is happening in our lives. We just have to learn how to tune our spiritual antennae to His frequency.

To do so, we have to practice going before Him and seeking His face to build that relationship. James 4:8 says, "Draw nigh to God, and He will draw nigh to you." We can't use God like a magical genie to grant us wishes whenever we want them and never give anything in return. Time with God also helps to fill up and renew our spirit from the trials and tribulations we face in life. It helps us to live out the Word that we should read daily. Most importantly, it helps us to know the direction God wants us to go in life. Even writing this book, I had to be still before the Lord to hear what He wanted me to write.

While you are processing emotions and seeking the Lord, there is one significant consideration you will have to keep in mind, and that is the necessity of guarding your mind and spirit. Be very selective about who is around you during this time. Please recognize that you might be in a mentally, emotionally, and spiritually vulnerable state. People you shouldn't be around are those who are users, abusers, negative Nancys, or anyone else who drains and pollutes your spirit. If you can't prevent them from being around you, then limit your interactions and communications with them. As mentioned earlier, you are in a more vulnerable state when you are working through deep-seated emotional issues, and you should try to be around people who support you, care about you, and most importantly, pour into you. Pray for God to shield you from those who do not add to you, and for Him to bring good people in your life.

After tearing down destructive strongholds in your heart and mind, there is a rebuilding period where you work toward being the person you want to be. Once you have cleaned out the past, you have to start preparing yourself for a healthy future. You have to be surrounded by positivity and things that make you feel happy and fulfilled. Never internalize rejection or ostracism, but instead carry around your peace like a purse and your resolve like a wallet. You should almost feel like you are in a protective bubble. You have to make an intentional effort to keep your peace and positivity.

During my period of self-healing, I used to put the revelations I learned on index cards on my wall. I had to be constantly exposed to those new thoughts until I internalized them. Put your new mental outlook in visible places so that you are constantly reminded to think positively. When someone insults or disrespects you, don't accept their assessment of you. There is room for you in this world; you don't have to make yourself smaller in anyone's presence. If anyone makes you feel otherwise, don't receive it. Explicitly reject it, either in your mind or out loud. For example, say, "I am not what ___ said, I am what God says I am."

After you have processed old hurts and have improved your thought life, it is time to learn how to enjoy the new and improved you! An important revelation for as someone who is a misfit, a weirdo, or an introvert to know is that you're going to spend more time alone than other people. Therefore, it is essential that you enjoy your own company! It may be hard in the beginning to accept that periods of loneliness may be a part of your journey, but you will learn that these periods are blessings in disguise. Acknowledge your loneliness and longingness when it comes instead of running to someone else to fulfill you. Mark Twain once said, "The worst loneliness is to not be comfortable with yourself."

The truth of the matter is that as a misfit, your self-esteem has probably taken a beating. You probably have spent many years being misunderstood, ridiculed, and rejected. Those experiences can be difficult to get over. Worst of all, you may have begun to treat yourself just as harshly as others have treated you. It has to be a deliberate learning and unlearning process to feel good about yourself. Once you have a good handle on who you are as a person and what you like, you have to learn how to be good to yourself. Be a lover of yourself. Take yourself to dinner. Dress nicely just because you want to feel attractive in your own eyes. Be kind to yourself and give yourself what you need. Give yourself permission to be imperfect, and have unconditional love for yourself. This attitude will free you from feeling needy or trying to earn someone's love in moments of loneliness. As a misfit, you will have to learn how to be nicer to yourself than anyone else.

If your self-esteem is not where it needs to be, now is the time to start building it up. If you reflect on your thought life, you will probably realize that you may think and say worse things about yourself than anyone around you. When I was younger, I would work hard at everything to try to make up for being so different. I used to push myself beyond the point of exhaustion, and I never gave myself the chance to make mistakes. If I did, I beat myself up pretty badly, and my self-esteem would take a nose dive. I was tense, fearful, paranoid, and miserable.

Additionally, I would work hard to please those around me by being "nice," overextending myself, and by essentially trying to buy love.

I had to work hard to get that weight of self-deprecation and self-sacrifice off of my back. When I finally did, I had never felt so light and free. It was a mind-boggling concept to know that I didn't have to work to feel like I had value. I had value by my mere existence! With this newfound freedom, I could then enter a new environment and not feel pressured to perform, be "on," or to be perfect. The easier it became to love and be kind to myself, the easier it was to be kind to and love others. Joy came naturally and easily, and I didn't feel the pressure to try to prove myself anymore. I was okay with people not liking me or understanding me because I finally knew my worth.

So when you enter a room, think about the love you have for yourself. Carry yourself with confidence and have a high opinion of yourself. When you enter a new environment, expect success. Isaiah 30:15 says, "In quietness and in confidence shall be your strength." Not to mention Proverbs 23:7, which says, "For as he thinketh in his heart, so is he." Knowing your worth is empowering, but truly thinking well of yourself will have a magical effect on your life. If you need to, meditate on scriptures that uplift you. Constantly feed your spirit positivity through things like books, music, internet sites, and by attending church. You can use multiple sources at one time; the sky is the limit!

As you are learning how to enjoy your own company, try new things. Learn a new skill or indulge in a new hobby. Enrich yourself, and add interest and value to yourself as a person. Whatever you do, let it be something you are genuinely interested in, or something that you've always wanted to do or learn. Create exciting goals for yourself and make your life as interesting as possible. Surround yourself with things you love and fill your life with all the things that make you happy. It could be colors, flowers, art, people, music, or anything else that brings you joy. You should also schedule treats for yourself on a regular basis. For example, establish a routine of weekly pedicures, monthly golf course visits, quarterly plays, or yearly trips. You have to start training yourself to be good to yourself, otherwise it's easy to forget. Activist Parker Palmer is quoted as saying, "Self-care is never a selfish act—it is simply good stewardship of the only gift I have, the gift I was put on earth to offer to others."

As part of embracing your newfound identity, it is important to continue resisting pressure to conform in a way that is not authentic to how you operate. Do only what you feel comfortable doing. For example, let's say both your mother and your favorite magazine tell you to approach men to ask for dates. However, if that's not your style and you don't feel comfortable doing it, you shouldn't do it. Once you accept the fact that you are different, you have to be adamant that others around you accept it as well. That is why a strong sense of self, as well as self-understanding and self-love, go such a long way in being successful. You can avoid the pitfalls of engaging in behaviors and activities that you know are not right for you.

What has always been frustrating for me, is feeling being pressured to do things in a specific manner. It wasn't that I couldn't do something, it was just sometimes I did it differently than others. For example, when I was a teacher, my natural teaching and classroom management style was different from many of my colleagues. A lot of other teachers focused on trying to be popular and having "fun" classes as a way to get the students to behave, but I felt it was important to focus on discipline and teaching them to strive for excellence. I know that if I had tried to win the students over by being the "cool" teacher, I would have failed because that tactic isn't authentic to my ideology and personality.

There will be times where you will have to learn how to manage those who might try to dim your newfound light. You must ensure that you do not let others steal your joy. Trust your gut about people and situations. That's one of the benefits of spending more time developing your spirit and mind—your intuition will become much stronger, and God will be able to speak to your spirit very clearly. Nowadays, before I accept an invitation somewhere, I pray. I know my light may be dimmed around certain atmospheres and individuals. Therefore, I need to know if the experience will be positive and edifying. Anything from volunteering to social meet-ups, concerts, and dates will not be accepted without prayerful consideration.

As you go through your journey of self-healing and self-discovery, it may seem like a long stretch of darkness to get through, but just like a tunnel, know that there is light and freedom at the end of it. At the end of the day, there are only two sources of love that can ever truly fill an empty heart. That is the love of God, and self-love. These are also the best kinds of love because with these two, no one on this earth has the power to take them away. As Oscar Wilde once said, "To love oneself is the beginning of a life-long romance."

Chapter Activity

It is important during your period of self-reflection that you examine your thought life very carefully. When you work to heal past wounds, you should be asking yourself very specific questions about your past. You should ask yourself these questions not only to uncover lingering hurts, but also to recognize harmful thoughts and behavior patterns. Your external world is a reflection of your internal thought world, and you attract what you think about the most. You have to change your thought life to change yourself and your life.

For instance, if you ever feel jealous, it may be an indication that you think there are limits on what *you* can receive. Our minds are restricted by what we are taught or assume, and we carry a long list of can'ts, don'ts, won'ts, and shouldn'ts for ourselves. Therefore, use these questions to help guide you to areas in your thought life you need to change.

- Do believe you deserve good things and good experiences? Examine why or why not.

- Do you view life with a jaded or pessimistic lens? If so, when did this start?

Also, pay attention to how you seek love. If you only got attention by crying, or when you were afraid, you have been trained to think that that you have to feel bad to get love. Ask yourself, when did you receive love as a child? Was it after an achievement, a failure, or when you were scared? These experiences affect how and when we expect love to manifest. It also affects what behaviors we exhibit to get it.

- To you feel like you have to earn love?

- Are you engaging in negative behaviors to receive love?

- What does love look like to you? Is this behavior a healthy display of love?

As you work through your issues, realize that your childhood can never be changed or repaired. Many of our issues have been kept secret from others, but we can't keep them secret from ourselves. You must acknowledge and face the emotions you have lingering from your childhood. We all have unconscious wounds we have not dealt with, and we are doomed to repeat these cycles if we do not confront our demons. Many of our behaviors and reactions could link back to unresolved childhood traumas.

- Do you react more severely to certain situations than you should? What situations in particular?

- Do you have trouble opening up because you never truly felt worthy of love, respect, and good things?

- Do you believe that if people knew the real you they wouldn't like you?

If you answered yes to any of these questions, then all of these thoughts and feelings must be acknowledged, confronted, and overcome. You have to figure out where the root of these feelings originates. Only by facing the past can we be free from it. When this is done, this will liberate your thoughts and emotions so that you may funnel them into more worthy pursuits. The memories of the past will then become fact-based and less emotionally-charged when you think of them. This journey may get intense and sometimes difficult, but please remember to stay joyful and positive throughout the process.

Start the process by congratulating yourself for overcoming and surviving all the obstacles in your life. Write down all the ways they have helped you to cope and succeed in life. Write fifty compliments about yourself. Be as flattering as possible. If you struggle with self-esteem issues, you might find it hard to find that many, but push yourself anyway. Ask those who love you what they like about you, and what your best qualities are if you get stuck. This exercise will force you to examine yourself differently. It will cause to see all the many great things there are about you, no matter how small. Put this list in a visible place to constantly remind yourself of what's great about you. Most of all, don't give up! God has a plan and a purpose for your life.

CHAPTER 4

Cliques Are Killers

"A 'normal person' is what is left after society has squeezed out all unconventional opinions and aspirations out of a human being."

—Mokokoma Mokhonoana

At least once in your life, you have experienced the desire to belong to a group. It could have been an exclusive group, a clique, a sorority or fraternity, a club, or athletic team. These desires are normal, but depending on the motivation behind those desires, joining specific groups may not be beneficial to misfits. If you are drawn to the aspirational or inspirational goals of the organizations, then that is a good sign you should pursue it. However, if you want to join to just to fit in, or to have a sense of value, then you should reconsider before proceeding.

Don't misunderstand me; a sense of belonging is very important to our sense of identity, as well as to our mental and emotional well-being. Yet great care must be exercised as to where and how we try to fit in.

When it comes to fitting in, there is a big difference between groups and cliques. Cliques can be found everywhere, from school to work and even church. In fact, cliques can even be found within larger groups. However, I have found that cliques are generally like very rigid boxes where those on the inside look down on those who are on the outside. They exist strictly for exclusionary purposes. Although the members can be united around shared ideologies, they are usually bound by superficial commonalities. Oftentimes, members mistakenly base their value on membership to said group. Members of cliques also spend a great deal of time adhering to unwritten rules about what's acceptable for their group to do. As I have stated before, a misfit who wants to be successful can't spend their life trying to be something that they aren't.

In addition to facing pressure to conform, cliques are dangerous because they can put you in the wrong company of people. You can easily get grouped in with the wrong people, and it could end up harming your reputation. Your circle of friends will either take you up or down. Very rarely will those you surround yourself with have little to no impact on your life. In extreme cases, they can alter the very course of your life. For example, former congressman and former president of the NAACP, Kweisi Mfume, spent time in jail as a youth because of those he surrounded himself around. He is quoted as saying, "Not only did I run with all the worst people, I became the leader." Had he not consciously decide to turn his life around, he would not have fulfilled his true purpose, nor would he have had the opportunity to impact the lives of millions of others.

Perhaps one of the biggest pitfalls of being a part of cliques or groups is the possibility of wasting time and energy on things not aligned to your destiny. You can become consumed with insignificant goals that do not help you become a better you. Not to mention that most misfits, weirdos, and introverts can be pretty inconsistent when it comes to social commitments. We often prefer alone time and can do quite well by ourselves. Making a commitment to a group means you have to be consistent with your communication and interactions with other members. You may have to attend events that you probably would have skipped if you weren't in the group, and you may have to cooperate with individuals you probably don't want to be around. If you know you can't or don't want to be consistent in interacting with others; then that is a sign that you are not ready to be a part of a group. I am not trying to discourage anyone from joining groups; I just want to make sure you are fully aware of what they entail so that you don't commitment yourself to something without knowing the cost. Being a part of a movement takes time, energy, and commitment, and if you aren't in a place to give that, it is better to wait until you are.

Before joining any group, be honest with yourself about your ability to handle these new relationships. Make a mental note of every time you change yourself to fit in. You could be tempted to subconsciously falling back on old thoughts and beliefs. We have to train ourselves to see when we are falling into old habits. Before trying to befriend someone, determine if this person will be good for you in the long run. Do their values and lifestyles align with yours in a beneficial way? How much does what others do and say influence your actions? If you feel susceptible to caving into peer pressure, you might want to limit who you are around until you have the mental and emotional strength to be yourself consistently. Additionally, if you find yourself constantly being sucked into the crowd, that means you need to take the focus off other people for a while and put it back on your own goals.

Develop yourself fully before trying to be a part of something. Only then will you have something to offer. Only when you know and enjoy who you are, can you bring a complete person to the table. Furthermore, you will also be less likely to feel intimidated or jealous of those around you because you are secure in yourself. Even if you are different from others, be secure in the unique assets you have to offer. You add value when you bring something different. You bring a new perspective, a new mentality, and fresh ideas. When you do decide to join a group, be not only interesting, but also be genuinely interested in those around you. Remember, people love those who love them.

If you have worked on you, but aren't ready for the commitment of a group, try focusing on finding genuine friendships instead. While you are searching, it is essential to keep in mind the importance of finding friends on your level. Maybe you didn't grow up with a silver spoon in your mouth, but you also didn't grow up in abject poverty either. Find friends that can relate to your journey and experiences. That doesn't mean you need to exclude people with different life experiences than yourself, but at a minimum, they should share the same values and ideologies as you. Choose friends who can be a support system to help you stay on track to achieve your goals. For example, if you want to remain strong in your faith, your friends should be mature Christians. If you want to excel in school, your friends should be academically successful; and if you want to be rich, your friends should either be rich, or at a minimum, have the same goal as you.

When connecting with others, your focus as a misfit, weirdo, or introvert is not to be a part of a clique, but to rather find your kind. Too many times, those of us who are different are surrounded by people who are nothing like us. This can be manageable, but it can also be wearisome and lonely. To combat unnecessary loneliness, you should actively try to "find your kind," meaning you should actively seek out those you have commonality with. It could be over a belief system, a lifestyle, interests, hobbies, causes, or anything else you can connect over. You can create a community of like-minded individuals that buoy your spirit, stimulate your mind, and enrich your soul. The size of your community doesn't matter. It can be two or 200. What matters is that there is mutual respect and acceptance. Barry Manilow is famously quoted as saying, "Misfits aren't misfits among other misfits."

For example, you could be in medical school to help the traditionally underserved, yet you find yourself surrounded by rich, out-of-touch brats who could care less about anything but the prestige of their profession. This kind of situation can be taxing for a kind-hearted, empathetic person. Therefore, your community should be a place where you go to recharge your sense of purpose and passion. Being around other empathic people will help your own empathy grow instead of weaken. At work, we have little control over who we spend our days with, but in your personal time, misfits must make sure that they are surround by people who understand and affirm them. Many times this support will be critical to facing the constant struggle to fit in and succeed in conventional workplaces.

If you are stuck on how to find your kind, start out small. For me, I found an online forum of like-minded women. I had a place where

I could interact with, and be inspired by, other women like me. You can go to meet-ups or join clubs with individuals with similar interests. We are lucky now that we can connect with so many diverse people through social media and the internet. Take advantage of it! It is one of the safest and easiest ways to connect with other people. There is a massive world out there, so don't be confined by your current environment or zip code.

When you are looking for your kind, don't settle. Be just as selective as others in who you choose to fill your inner circle with. There are real consequences to connecting with the wrong people. If you are in a period of success in your life, you will draw people to you regardless of if you are a misfit. Proverbs 19:4 says, "Wealth attracts many friends." However, not all of these people will have your best interests in mind. Some will come to see what they can get, some will come to see how to trip you up, but there will be some who will come into your life because they are attracted to the real you. Use the low periods of your life to see who truly has your back. Caution is necessary because those closest to you are in the position to hurt you the most.

Additionally, if you discover that you are in a clique that you realize you are in for the wrong reasons, you should take steps to slowly remove yourself from that clique. I have found that getting negative people out of your life is not an overnight process. It might take months or years, and sometimes, they may never completely disappear. This is one of the reasons why it is so important to proceed with caution when adding new people in your life. It can be extremely painful and difficult to disentangle them from your life later.

I think that it is also key to talk about relationships under this topic because some of the reasons we try to fit into cliques are the same reasons we jump into relationships. The appeal of someone new may say more about your own neediness than about the charm of the other person. You have to search for the real meaning of why you want to be in a relationship. It could be due to societal pressures, the fear of being alone, wanting love, sexual fulfillment, or just a sign of social status. Look at your current relationship or your relationships in the past. Was there an underlying reason you decided to be with this person? If you find yourself in a current relationship that you know you are in for the wrong reasons, you will have to treat this relationship the same as you would an unsuitable clique.

One chief difference between leaving a clique versus a relationship is that at the end of the relationship, you should give yourself enough time to mourn it. You should mourn it with self-nurture and self-protection. This should also be done without the aid of artificial tranquilizers and numbing agent such as food, drugs, alcohol, sex, shopping, or anything else that you use in a negative way to cope with your feelings. Make no impulsive decisions during this time. Acknowledge the feelings you have toward the person, but realize you should no longer have to act on them. It is normal for memories, regrets, desire for revenge, as well as a real sense of loss, to far outlast the relationship. Just know that these feelings won't last forever. In fact, I am sure you can think of at least one relationship that when you look back on it, you wonder why you ever wanted that person in your life in the first place! In the end, just acknowledge your feelings, process them, and move on.

If you are having trouble finding your kind, stay encouraged and hopeful. Something interesting that I found is that many of the cliques and groups that reject you actually do you a favor. Sometimes misfits are rejected because they stand out, but the very thing that makes them stand out will eventually be the source of their success. You should know that a door closing is more an elimination of paths that are not for you, rather than a symbol of your worth or value. For instance, Steven Spielberg was rejected by his first choice film school *twice*. Yet he went on to become one of the most renowned filmmakers in the world. No one knows what kind of director he would have been had he attended USC. Perhaps he would have changed his style to fit the viewpoint of the school he was so enamored with. In the end, just know that rejection can be just as much of a blessing as an acceptance can be.

Your mindset moving forward should be to have people serve as inspiration in your life and not as a crutch. Public acceptance will never replace self-love. No group membership will create, add to, or dictate your value. If you are going to join a group, constantly remind yourself that you can be united in the mission without having to be exactly like the person beside you. What you have to offer is valuable, so don't join any group that doesn't recognize that.

Chapter Summary

Most times when we feel the need to fit in and join cliques, it is because we fear being alone. We don't want to be reminded of how unlovable we feel, we don't want to feel bad about ourselves, or we don't want to face social situations alone. At times, we have this desire because we think we need the validation of other people. Yet you must understand that there are some needs no human can fill. These needs can only be filled by God, and truly loving and accepting yourself as you are.

When considering joining a group, it isn't a question of if joining a group is good, but rather finding the group that is best for you. As a misfit, weirdo, or introvert, you're probably better off with a smaller group of friends, mainly because there is always a stronger pressure to conform in a larger group of people. One of the challenges of being a misfit is that you are different; therefore, there will always be others who can't relate to you. When you are in larger group settings, you will feel pressure to suppress those differences in order to blend in. Yet smaller groups will allow for a more intimate setting that allows you to open up in a more authentic manner.

Lastly, look at the relationships you have at present. It is important to identify if there are any negative relationships in your life. Know every relationship will involve some type of hurt. Proverbs 27:6 says, "Faithful are the wounds of a friend." Damaged feelings can be processed, worked through, and minimized; but when pain is frequent or severe, it is abuse. Those relationships need to be ended immediately. For real and positive relationships, recognize that they need to be nurtured properly in order to bear fruit. If you don't have the time or stamina to interact with others for an extended period of time, you're not ready yet to be a part of a group. Wait until you have the mental and emotional fortitude to fulfill the commitments of being a group member.

If you are not ready for a group, work on building strong friendships instead. The truth is that it is the not quantity of friends you have that matters, but the quality. You can do more with two real friends than 200 superficial ones. Proverbs 18:24 says, "A man who has friends must himself be friendly, But there is a friend who sticks closer than a brother." Who you surround yourself around matters, so choose carefully!

CHAPTER 5

top Trying to Understand the "Why"

"O Lord, help me not to despise or oppose what I do not understand."

—William Penn

Many, many times in my life, I have cried out to God for answers on why my life was the way it was. Sometimes I was angry, sometimes I was hurt, and at other times I was scared. I wanted to understand why my life and I were so complicated; I wanted to know why my journey had so many twists, turns, and obstacles. Why did everything seem to fall into place for those around me, while I had to fight and claw for everything and make it by the skin of my teeth? Time and time again, I never got an answer, yet I was always given peace and comfort to help me through those moments. More recently, when I ask God this same question, he answered very clearly in my spirit with two words: "Keep going." When I received those words, they were accompanied by both a sense of urgency and correction. I knew then that I was no longer allowed to feel self-pity or sadness about my circumstances.

Now I understand it was imperative to stop looking back and to put all of my energy into the future in order for me to reach my full potential. The Lord made it very clear to me that my present actions mattered way more than anything that happened in the past, so I had to focus. I still don't know why certain events have transpired in my life. I don't know why I have been so different even from a young age, and quite frankly, I may never know. However, what I do know is that there is a reason, and I can only receive what God wants for me by following the path that He has lain out for me.

Looking back, the real reason why I would cry out to God so often was because the thought of being different was simply terrifying to me. I didn't want to spend my entire life sticking out like a sore thumb. Perhaps you share the same fears. Well, rest assured that you are not alone. Jesus' own followers couldn't figure out why they faced so much trouble. Paul is quoted as saying in 2 Corinthians 4:8-9, "We are hard pressed on every side, but not crushed; perplexed, but not in despair; persecuted, but not abandoned; struck down, but not destroyed." Though he faced trouble, he knew that trusting God was what was more important than trusting in his own wisdom. Solomon, the wisest king to ever walk the face of the earth, also understood this important principle when he wrote, "Trust in the Lord with all your heart, and lean not on your own understanding" in Proverbs 3:5.

Furthermore, trying to figure out the "why" takes time and focus off your purpose. It can put you in a negative state of mind as it keeps you looking backwards instead of forward. More important for you than the "why" is the "when" of the purpose of your life colliding with the authentic manifestation of yourself. You should be actively seeking and working toward the place you need to be and not looking back to where you have been. When your focus is on where you are going, you don't have time to feel sorry about your past. Precious time and energy are lost over things that can't be changed. Focus on what you do have control over now.

Asking "why" also puts us in the unfortunate position of potentially being jealous of those around us. When we ask "why," we assume that our lives should look like those of the people around us. We look at others whose lives seem perfect, but we have no idea about the hidden struggles they face. Perhaps you have even been a victim of someone who was jealous of your seemingly perfect life. You know all too well what can lurk beneath a shiny surface. Just know that the root of jealousy is almost always low self-esteem. You become jealous when you feel like someone has something you can't get yourself. If you truly felt like you could have those things, you would just work towards getting them. However, since you feel like you can't have them, those unmet desires turn into jealousy. Since you have no idea what others are going through, you should never be jealous of them. You don't know their struggles, scars, or secrets, so focus on what is meant for you.

I sincerely believe that we face obstacles in life because God gives us tests and lessons to help prepare us for the work that He has for us. Those life experiences guide you toward the work you are meant to do. Romans 8:28 says, "We know that in all things God works for the good of those who love Him, who have been called according to His purpose." There are many situations that when they occurred, I was hurt and angry, but now I can look back on them and see what a valuable lesson they taught me about either myself, others, or life. In fact, I think I am a more well-rounded and compassionate person because of the suffering I have endured.

Famous financial guru Suze Orman worked as a waitress for seven years. During those years, she would often tell her regular customers about her dream to open a spa one day. One day, a regular wrote her a check to do just that. She managed to raise $50,000 from friends and well-wishers to open her business. She took the money to Merrill Lynch to have it invested, but her assigned representative promptly lost all of it in very risky investments. Instead of being bitter about her misfortune, she decided to learn how to become an investor and applied to work at Merrill Lynch. She got the job, and the rest is history. She didn't take her setback as a sign that she couldn't succeed, nor did she cry and ask "why me?" Instead, she used that same company that lost her money to help her make millions more.

When asked why she took the steps she did, she said, "You know, the truth is when your back is up against the wall, when you owe somebody something—sometimes you won't do something for yourself, but when you need to do something for somebody else to pay them back, you owe them, you lost what they gave you, that gives you the courage." Use your setbacks and failures as motivation to know that you are a survivor and that you can pick yourself up and move forward, no matter the obstacle.

I believe the biggest reason why God doesn't tell us everything is because He wants us to trust Him. In Hebrews 11:6, it says "And without faith it is impossible to please God, because anyone who comes to Him must believe that He exists and that He rewards those who earnestly seek Him." God wants to help you. However, He can't if you don't surrender your control to Him. Isaiah 55:8-9 says, "'For my thoughts are not your thoughts, neither are your ways my ways,' declares the Lord. 'As the heavens are higher than the earth, so are my ways higher than your ways, and my thoughts than your thoughts.' For His ways are higher than our ways." Therefore, if we truly believe and understand how omniscient, omnipresent, and omnipotent God is, we should know He is better equipped to lead our life than we are.

We should constantly seek God to make the best decisions of our lives. 1 Thessalonians 5:17 says "to pray without ceasing" and Proverbs 3:6 says, "In all thy ways acknowledge Him, and He shall direct thy paths." God doesn't want us to walk through this life blindly, but rather, He wants us to come to Him for guidance for the best path to take. In Jeremiah 29:11, God's messages to us is, "'For I know the plans I have for you,' declares the Lord, 'plans to prosper you and not to harm you, plans to give you hope and a future.'" If we truly believe that, then we must pray, believing that God will guide us to where he wants us to be. Too often, we try to figure out thing and do things on our own, and when we fail, we blame God. God clearly wants us to succeed, but we must follow His way in order to receive His blessings.

Though you may not know why specific things in your life occur, that doesn't mean that God won't give us understanding. It also doesn't mean we should go through life blindly, without trying to understand ourselves and the world around us. God wants us to have wisdom and understanding. Proverbs 2:6 says, "For the Lord giveth wisdom: out of His mouth cometh knowledge and understanding."

Knowledge is critical to anyone who wants success, and thankfully, it is not just limited to the classroom. Many successful individuals learned from the School of Hard Knocks, others from observing their peers, while quite a few are self-taught. There is no limit to how and where you can be educated. You can learn in school, at work, church, at play, and you can learn from books, people, the internet, and just about any other medium there is.

When I was a teacher, I felt I learned just as much from the students as they learned from me. I learned about new perspectives, pop culture, and most importantly, human behavior. Proverbs 18:15 says, "The heart of the prudent getteth knowledge; and the ear of the wise seeketh knowledge."

Alternatively, you have to be careful what you are feeding your mind. Just as with feeding your body, you can feed your mind either junk or substance. If you read four romance novels a week but never pick up a book that helps you to improve your life, you have a mental diet of fast food. By watching trashy reality TV shows you can subconsciously desensitize yourself to negative behavior. When you are confronted with these types of behavior in real life, you may not react appropriately because you are so used to seeing it on TV. Make sure that what you are feeding your mind is what is beneficial to you in the end. Just as with junk food, some things are okay with moderation, but you should never fill your mind and spirit up with only junk. Career coach Dan Miller recommends spending two hours a day reading inspirational material. No matter what time limit you choose, you should be constantly working to develop your mind and spirit.

With every experience you have in life, make it a point to learn something new from it. With this mentality, you can avoid repeating destructive cycles in your life as well as rebound from failure much quicker. This approach will also help you to help others who can't see the lessons in their own lives. In fact, you will find it is a blessing to share the wisdom you have learned to help others make it through their own difficult moment. Also having a thoughtful and reflective disposition will teach you how to be objective in seeing your own flaws. It is only when we see and acknowledge our flaws that we can fix them. When combined, all of these actions will make you an infinitely better person who has an incredible amount of wisdom to contribute to the world.

Chapter Summary

At times it may feel as if we are helpless to what happens to us, and that things happen without rhyme or reason. Rest assured that no matter how choppy the sea gets or how the wind blows, Jesus is on the boat. Nothing you have gone through has been in vain. God will use every circumstance for His glory. We just have to surrender our lives to His will and to trust Him to lead us to our best. Therefore, when God gives us direction, we have to listen.

Though we have blind trust in God, that does not mean we have to go through life blindly. God will give us wisdom and understanding to help us navigate life. James 1:5 says, "If you need wisdom, ask our generous God, and He will give it to you. He will not rebuke you for asking." It is then up to you to seek knowledge and understanding so that you live in abundance and success. Constantly seek to understand and to obtain new knowledge. Read, learn, and improve. God gave us intelligence and free will for a reason. He has given us the tools and the authority to walk in victory; we just have to use them. The Bible is our life manual, so we should constantly refer to it to make the best decisions possible.

Finally, focus your energy on the future and not the past. Focusing on the "why" of our past only leaves us facing the wrong direction. Wondering "why" also affirms the false expectation that our lives will look like those of the people around us. It can trap us into feeling resentful and jealous. Ultimately, our future success will depend on what we do with the things we have control over, and not on things we cannot change and events that have already passed us by.

CHAPTER 6

Change Your Scent

"We can easily forgive a child who is afraid of the dark; the real tragedy of life is when men are afraid of the light."

—Plato

One factor that contributes to the isolation of misfits, weirdos, and introverts is our propensity to approach new environments with fear. Unfortunately, people can smell fear. Fear makes you more awkward than you already are because it shows in your demeanor and words. It kills your confidence and turns you into a shell of who you really are. It's a thief that steals your joy, your hope, and your dreams, and then paralyzes you while you helplessly watch all the good drain from your life.

Of course, the fact that you shouldn't be scared doesn't take away the fact your fears may be real. Perhaps you have been rejected in a very painful way in the past, and those scars have turned into fear. Though your fears may not be unfounded, constantly fearing rejection is doing more harm for you than good. I have discovered that the two most destructive emotions humans have are anger and fear. Anger makes you outwardly destructive, while fear makes your internally destructive.

It destroys your self-esteem as well as your sense of security. For this reason alone, it is time to erase those fears so that you can live life to its fullest potential.

One of the easiest ways to overcome fear to find something you love more than you fear it. For "there is no fear in love. But perfect love drives out fear, because fear has to do with punishment. The one who fears is not made perfect in love," according to 1 John 4:18.

If you feel lonely, just know that fear is the only obstacle to love. When we spend so much time being scared of rejection, we are not in a place to open our hearts to receive love. Start by doing something you've been scared to do. It could be traveling alone, joining a group, or public speaking. This is not to say that you won't have moments of fear, the key is not to let it rule you. Acknowledge the fear, but still act anyway. It is easy to talk yourself out of doing things because of fear, but just get into the habit of acting anyway. If fear is the only reason why you don't want to do something, just know that that is not a good reason not to do it.

When things scare you, practice running to them, not away from them. What you are really running away from is fear. This isn't to say you should block out real dangers and warning signals, but rather, when something feels too big or good for you, you should stop running away from it. The sad reality is that most people are more afraid of good possibilities than bad possibilities. So many times in my life, I have shied away from opportunities because I was scared of rejection or not being good enough. Ellen Johnson-Sirleaf, the first female President of Liberia, is quoted as saying, "If your dreams don't scare you, then they are not big enough." Remember that as you move closer and closer to your destiny.

Perhaps the most significant thing you need to remember as you try to overcome fear is that you don't have to be afraid because God is with you. Fear equals a lack of faith. Learn to depend on Him. Psalms 27:1 says, "The Lord is my light and my salvation; whom shall I fear? The Lord is the strength of my life; of whom shall I be afraid?" Psalms 27:3 goes even further by saying, "Even if an army gathers against me, my heart will not be afraid. Even if war rises against me, I will be sure of You." If we learn to put our confidence in God, and not in ourselves, then we know that we have no reason to fear others. 2 Timothy 1:7 says, "For God hath not given us the spirit of fear; but of power, and of love, and of a sound mind." God makes it very clear that living in fear is not His desire for us. Take His Word and know that you can use His love to drive out fear.

If you feel like you like you are constantly facing the same situations that cause you fear, it may be God's way of forcing you to address this problem, so you are not held back when it is time to fulfill your purpose. You may have attracted someone in your life to show you what your hidden fears are. Use those encounters to practice facing and overcome your fear instead of letting it control you. View your fear as a way to announce a threat, an unresolved issue, or as a warning that something may not be right. Once you view fear as a sign of an unsolved issue, then you can start focusing your attention on figuring out how to resolve the root cause. Ancient Chinese philosopher Lao Tzu is quoted as saying, "He who knows others is wise. He who knows himself is enlightened." You should always understand and be aware of where your fear originates.

Another key factor to overcoming fear is to change your thought life. Stop playing the worst case scenario in your mind. Philippians 4:8 says, "Finally, brethren, whatsoever things are true, whatsoever things are honest, whatsoever things are just, whatsoever things are pure, whatsoever things are lovely, whatsoever things are of good report; if there be any virtue, and if there be any praise, think on these things." Visualize the best and most ideal outcome before starting any endeavor. Visualize a resolution before the problem is fixed. Visualize a good situation, and every time you start to worry about the problem, visualize a positive ending. Immediately change negative thoughts to positive ones when they enter your mind. Thank God in advance for your pending success. Monitoring your thought life is one of the most important things you can do to overcome fear. This is because your thoughts affect your actions, and your actions will determine your outcome.

Besides positive thinking, there are actions you can take to be better prepared to face new environments. Having an action plan for encountering new situations can help you not feel so defenseless against others' reactions to and perceptions of you. There is some awkwardness about yourself that you can fix. For example, a young Warren Buffet was terrified of public speaking and often vomited at the thought of doing it. He spent years rearranging his life so he wouldn't ever have to speak publicly. Then one day he decided to face his worst fear. He took a class on public speaking offered by the author of the critically-acclaimed book *How to Win Friends and Influence People*, Dale Carnegie. In addition to the class, Buffett taught himself other tricks to help him with his public speaking. Now he has successful speaking engagements all over the world.

I remember when I joined the Diplomatic Corps. I completely underestimated the amount of networking, meet and greets, and downright schmoozing events we were expected to attend. As an introvert, I hate networking events! However, I had to learn how to start and hold conversations with complete strangers on a regular basis. What helped me to do this was to view those events as work (as they were) instead of social events. It was easier to process and handle this task when I viewed it as a job. Additionally, I tried not to reflect on my own personal fears and insecurities, but rather put all of my attention on the other person. As the conversation developed, I started to become engrossed in the subject matter, and I completely forgot about my fear and loathing of the activity. Also, starting out with one-on-one conversations was easier to handle than group conversations. With each event, my comfort and confidence with the activity increased. I still do not like to go to networking events, but at least now I know how to handle them when I do have to go.

Another way to overcome fear is by failing faster. Robert Kiyosaki of the famed *Rich Dad, Poor Dad* book series wrote a book call *Before You Quit Your Job*. In that book, he says that when he was struggling to be a good salesman at Xerox, his rich dad told him to "fail faster." What his rich dad meant was that the more he failed, the more he would learn from those mistakes and get better. Therefore, if he wanted to get better faster, he had to fail faster. With this approach, failing becomes a form of practice that helps you get better at something. That advice resonated with me because I realized even if I faced my fears, that didn't stop me from failing. However, failing did stop me from being afraid to fail. By failing often, I realized that failure was not the end of the world, and I would live to see another day.

For example, I joined the ROTC program in the second semester of my freshman year in college. I was incredibly awkward and shy, and I hated being the center of attention—not exactly great characteristics to be successful in what essentially was a leadership program. I would do everything that was asked of me, but I did not reach out and make connections with the other cadets in the program. At the end of the year, we were asked to make a list of which cadet we wanted to lead us, ranking all of the freshman cadets in order. Well, when the results came back, I was dead last on everyone's list. Ouch, that hurt! Sensing my sadness, another cadet tried to cheer me up. He said, "Don't take it personal, everyone just listed their friends first." Although he was right, I still had not displayed any leadership abilities.

My sophomore year, I was thrust into various leadership roles because that was the nature of the program. I remember my first time I had to lead a formation. My voice wavered, and my body actually shook. I literally thought I was going to pass out from fear! Some of my classmates chuckled at my exaggerated reaction, but at the time, it was literally one of the scariest things I had ever done. Over and over again, I was forced to lead a formation or group. Little by little, my courage and confidence increased until I had drill and ceremony down pat. I even came to love singing Army cadence as I led groups of cadets to and from different locations on campus. As I progressed through the program, one higher-ranking cadet remarked about how far I had come from my initially shaky start, pun intended. I had faced my fear of being in front, and practiced until I could lead a group, no matter how big. By my senior year in college, I was the highest-ranking cadet in the entire program, and I graduated as a Distinguished Military Graduate. Not bad for the girl who started out being voted dead last for leadership ability!

I tell that story not to brag, but to rather say that I didn't accomplish all this because I was a natural born leader. Quite the opposite, in fact. There were many times where I was either too hard or too soft as a leader, and let me tell you, my peers did not hesitate to let me know when I was either! I remember trying to make a cadet drop and do push-ups, and her flat-out refusing. I also remember not speaking up because I was scared to voice an unpopular opinion. I learned that leading your peers is one of the hardest things you can be asked to do, but if you can master that, leading those under you is a breeze.

Overall in ROTC, I had failed many times. However, those failures allowed me the opportunity to fail faster. Consequently, by the time I was commissioned officer in the U.S. Army, I was able lead without visibly shaking in front of my platoon. I am forever grateful to the Battalion Commander, who consistently put me in leadership positions, even though I showed no outward potential. It was through those opportunities to fail that I learned how to lead.

Chapter Activity

The first step to overcoming fear is to recognize when you are acting out of fear. Are your goals, actions, and thoughts based on fear, or love? Are you pursuing a career in finance because you love it, or is it because you are scared about pursuing your dreams of being a chef?

What choices would you make if you were not afraid? Start by listing your fears (even the ones you are afraid to speak aloud—i.e., "my parents don't love me"). Most of the time, it is only when we write down and acknowledge our fears that we realize how irrational they are.

It is key to understand your fears because old fears trigger new fears. For example, you will start to say things like, "I knew ... would happen." Always be aware where your fears are rooted. When you know not only what your fear is, but why you have that fear, you can say things like, "This is a childhood fear of mine, but I now know that fear isn't true." You have to develop adult responses to childhood fears. For example, when people raise their hand around you, do you flinch because you were hit excessively as a child? You don't have to relive childhood trauma the rest of your life. Make a choice to break those mental chains you have been a slave for years.

Fear is an illogical way of protecting ourselves against what no longer threatens us. Our irrational fears tell us about past traumas we have not properly dealt with yet. You can even fear your own ability to handle your emotions and how powerless you may feel. For example, it is not stress that hurts you, but your inability to handle it. Your sense of helplessness is one of the most damaging feeling you have. A great book on understanding and processing fear is *When Love Meets Fear* by David Richo.

Think about how many times a day or week you relive old memories. Do you freeze up in certain situations? More importantly, can you pinpoint why? Write down every time you feel overwhelmed when it happens. Are there patterns? Also, write down any obsessive or compulsive thoughts and behavior. In these lists, if you have identified major fears that severely affect your ability to function, please reach out for help. There is no shame in seeking help if you need it. All counseling is confidential, and you don't have to share the fact that you are getting help if you don't want to. You will always feel fear—you just don't have to be a slave to it, nor do you have to face it alone.

CHAPTER 7

Be Weirder

"You're incredibly, absolutely, extremely, supremely, unbelievably different."

—Kami Garcia, Beautiful Creatures

Yes, you read that right. I said *be weirder*. What I mean is that you should start to express yourself the way you have always wanted to. Stop suppressing parts of yourself to fit it. Suppressing even the smallest aspect of yourself can hinder the complete fulfillment of your purpose. There is an explicit reason for everything about you. You were uniquely designed, and you were given specific attributes and traits for the work that only you were meant to do.

If you're worried that the people around you will not accept you, don't. Remember, fear in and of itself is never a valid reason not to do something. You have to take steps to move toward the most genuine, best you, whether others around you are ready for it or not. If you wait for others' approval, you will never be the person you were divinely appointed to be. Remember: find your kind instead of changing yourself to fit into the crowd.

If you are surrounded by judgmental people, just know that they are never going to understand your life journey, much less any inward or outward changes you are making. In the Biblical story of David and Saul, people used superficial attributes to determine who they thought should be king, including God's own prophet, Samuel! 1 Samuel 16:7 says, "But the Lord said to Samuel, 'Do not consider his appearance or his height, for I have rejected him. The Lord does not look at the things people look at. People look at the outward appearance, but the Lord looks at the heart.'" God doesn't use superficial criteria to determine our worth, so neither should you.

Differences are not just limited to appearances. Let's say you are a young man who loves to sing, but you live in a small football town. You may feel pressure to the "manly" sports star when in your heart all you want to do is sing with your guitar. Perhaps you come from a family of accomplished professionals, but your heart is not in white-collar work. Though you face pressure to conform, you can't let your present surroundings stop you from realizing your true destiny. Iconic *Vogue* editor Anna Wintour was fired from her job as a junior fashion editor at *Harper's Bazaar* for creating work that was too edgy. Imagine if she had suppressed her progressive and provocative eye for fashion editorials just to fit in. She has literally ushered in, exposed, and influenced fashion trends around the world!

You may think that standing out even more will make your life exponentially more difficult, but I have found that it is quite the opposite. Once you are living, thinking, and behaving in a way that feels natural to you, you will find it easier to handle what life throws your way. Trying to live like someone else is like trying to fight with your hands tied—you have so many restrictions that prevent you from moving in a natural way that it makes the fight more difficult than it has to be.

Additionally, being authentic helps increase your joy, not only because you are not living behind masks, but because you are also freeing your mind to focus on what's important to you versus focusing on how not to be. Perhaps one of the most unexpected ways your life will improve is that the act of being authentic will help expedite getting the wrong people out of your life. If you are pretending to be someone you are not and you finally let your authentic self come through, those who only wanted to see you one way will not remain. Instead, you will attract understanding people who relate to you and enjoy you for you.

Additionally, by exhibiting the courage to be yourself, people may admire your bravery. They might wish they had the courage to do the things you do. Many people are imprisoned in lives that they think they ought to live a certain way. They wish they could do what you are doing, but unfortunately, their fear of rejection and their need for security are much stronger impulses. The reality is that you can help others to be free when you become free yourself. By being yourself, you are giving others permission to be themselves as well. They will know that you are not expecting them to be anything other than who they truly are because you don't even put that expectation on yourself. There is a quote that says, "Butterflies can't see their wings. They can't see how beautiful they are, but everyone else can. People are like that as well." When you show your true self, you are showing others the beauty of your wings. And when others see the sight of your beauty, that will cause them to seek their own.

When you do encounter those who try to make you feel bad about yourself, just remember to protect your mind and spirit. Use some of the techniques discussed in Chapter 3 to help surround yourself with positivity. It will be a constant challenge for misfits to resist the temptation to fit in, but the outcome will be worth the effort. You can't rely on the opinions of superficial people to determine your value or what is best for you. Just recall that every person who changed the world did it by doing something everyone around them was unwilling to do. Therefore, when you focus on being a leader and not a follower, it will help you to put less stock in the opinions of others.

As stated before, self-expression is not just accomplished outwardly. Your difference may be in a vision for your life that is different from those around you. One word of caution, however, as you work toward being the person you want to be—and living the life you want to live— is not to forget to live in the moment. Even if you can't live your life exactly the way you envisioned it yet, don't put life on hold. I love to travel, and even though I didn't always have someone to travel with, that has not stopped me from traveling both domestically and internationally. If you are waiting for A, B, or C to be perfect before you say, buy a house, go back to school, or change careers, you may never get to do those things.

Some other things to be mindful of as you are working toward your goals is to work at your own pace, and to only do what you feel comfortable doing. This is a vital lesson to moving in your own space. Sometimes when we have goals, we are in a rush to accomplish them. However, whatever goal you have, you have to work at your own pace and not try to keep up with those around you. Just like the rules for success are different for misfits, so is the timing and pacing of the success. You can't look at how quickly others are doing something as a gauge for your own timeline. Go at the speed that feels comfortable for you.

When I was an undergraduate, I wanted to experience college like the other students around me. Academically, I could more than keep up, but socially, I was very much behind. I wanted to hang out, date, make lots of friends, and pledge. However, I was not emotionally and socially prepared to do those things the same way or at the same pace that my peers were. When I focused on what I could do, however, doors began to open for me. Although I wasn't invited to parties on Saturday nights, I had a core group of friends that I hung out with in the dorm instead. We watched TV, listened to music, and laughed our heads off. So though I wasn't at parties on Saturday night, my weekends were still a blast.

I also didn't experience the casual dating and hook-ups that my peers did. My first two years of college, I probably only went on about three dates. However, in my junior year, I met a very nice guy who I dated for about two and a half years. Although I did not pledge a Greek-letter sorority, I pledged a military one, and I have amazing memories from my times with those ladies.

I tell this story to show you that although my college experience did not mirror those of my peers, I still was able to enjoy it by moving at my own pace and working at my own level. By starting small, I gradually developed the social skills I had previously lacked, and I used those experiences to help me better navigate the social situations I would encounter in the future.

Maybe your dream is to be a global tech entrepreneur, but perhaps you don't have the network and contacts to get the venture capital for your business idea. Just start where you are. Start with a smaller, easier product that you can get funded and developed. Build your business with that idea and use the profits to help build the other great ideas you couldn't fund previously. The experience of building a business will become essential for launching your big idea, and the network and contacts you have built can help you grow it to the level that you have always wanted it to be. It isn't about how you start, but about how you finish. Zechariah 4:10 says, "Do not despise these small beginnings, for the Lord rejoices to see the work begin."

When you move on your level, you will find success comes more easily and naturally. You will also find that your growth will be organic to who you are as a person. You have to start with where you are, and doing what is natural and comfortable for you. You can call this "staying in your lane." Oprah started out on the evening news, but that wasn't comfortable for her. She would often cry on live television because of the heartbreaking stories she covered. She eventually ended up "demoted" to the morning show, and the rest, as you know, is history.

Another reason why pacing is important is because haste makes waste. If you feel a need to hurry to have something, it is a good sign you are pursuing it for the wrong reason. Your real motive might be to compete with others or prove yourself to them in some way; neither of which will not be beneficial for your unique path to success. Anything done hastily, from get-rich-quick schemes to marrying the first person who says "yes," are all ways to harm your future. Proverbs 21:5

says, "The plans of the diligent lead to profit as surely as haste leads to poverty."

There was a time in college where I didn't stay in my lane, and deviating showed me just how important it was to stay in my lane. It was during my senior year, and I felt a lot of pressure to buy a car. I really didn't have the money to spare at that time, so I took from my book money. Long story short, the car I arranged to buy I had to give back because I couldn't come up with the rest of the money. Since I had spent most of my book money for the down payment, I failed a class that I didn't have the book for. I was embarrassed and angry at myself for being so stupid. I had never failed a class, and I could have easily passed the class if I had the book. However, it was a lesson learned. I saved my money and the next semester I was able to buy a car without financial strain.

Sometimes you might feel the need to set goals for yourself on your journey. This is great, but try not stick to some unrealistic timeline of when they need to be accomplished. If you are living your life by some artificial timeline, stop! Your life has not looked like those around you, so why should the timeline of your milestones look the same? Don't feel pressure to attend college at a certain age, marry and have kids by a certain age, or start a business at a certain age. Your life was meant to be different!

In today's society, it is easy to develop a "Spoiled Milk" mentality. People, woman especially, have been trained to view themselves like a carton of milk that loses its value after a certain period of time. We think that as we age, the less desirable and valuable we are to society and potential partners. We dread the aging process because it represents the loss of our value and opportunities. If you think like this, please rid yourself of this mentality immediately!

People, especially women, get so much better as they age. They are smarter, funnier, and more interesting. The simple truth is that you actually have much more to offer to a marriage at age forty than at twenty because you have lived life and can bring so much more to the table. You have developed a true circle of friends, hobbies, life experience, money, stability, and most importantly, maturity. You come as a complete person and can enter the union without worrying about "what ifs." Even those who have children later in life bring so much more to the table as parents. When you think about your age and its relevance to your value, always think of yourself of as an ever-improving fine wine.

Chapter Summary

This is your life, and you should live it to the fullest. There is no way you can truly enjoy your life if you spend it hiding who you really are. You should not suppress any part of yourself just to fit in. It doesn't matter if is how you think or how you dress—your destiny is tied up in the uniqueness that God has placed in you. By living in the freedom of being an individual, you not only give others permission to be themselves, but you also will experience more personal contentment than ever before.

As you are working toward the life you want to have, learn to work at your own pace and within your own timeline. Trying to keep up with others is the best way to end up frustrated and unhappy. As a misfit, you have to learn how to not only accept a different journey, but also how to enjoy the ride until you reach your final destination. Don't hold off on living while you're waiting for your moment. Life doesn't have to be perfect in order for you to claim success. Celebrate the small victories to help sustain you until you get to the big ones.

Moving forward, practice taking the hurry out of your life. Think about all the things you can't do when you're in a hurry—talking to people, praying, being patient, listening, enjoying your food, taking in the scenery, or just dealing with less stress. All of these things are important to your mental and physical health. Take note of the things you see, feel, and hear on a day you are not in a rush. Are you missing the voice of God in the hustle and bustle?

When you work towards a goal, start slow and with whatever you have been given. Remember, Ecclesiastes 7:8 says, "Better is the end of a thing than the beginning thereof: and the patient in spirit is better than the proud in spirit."

CHAPTER 8

Don't Live Behind B.A.R.s

"Every villain is a hero in his own mind."

—Tom Hiddleston

Every day, I pray to God to deliver me from being trapped behind B.A.R.s. It is the most singular struggle that I have had. B.A.R.s stands for Bitterness, Anger, and Resentment. If you are holding onto to any of these three emotions, then you are living behind B.A.R.s.

There may be many reasons why you feel these emotions, and some will be more valid than others. Regardless, we will only experience these emotions if we feel wronged.

To be clear, bitterness, anger, and resentment are all related. Anger turns into resentment, which is persistent ill will at a perceived wrong, and resentment turns into bitterness, which is a chronic and pervasive state of smoldering resentment. Regardless of where you might be on this cycle, God is very clear about us not holding on to these emotions. Ephesians 4:31-32 says, "Get rid of all bitterness, rage and anger, brawling and slander, along with every form of malice. Be kind and compassionate to one another, forgiving each other, just as Christ God forgave you."

Everyone has experienced anger at some point or another, but resentment and bitterness are less understood. In addition to perceived wrongs, resentment can represent an unacknowledged sense of entitlement. You feel like you should have gotten the promotion, the woman, the client, or an elected position. Being aware of what your real feelings are will be the key to preventing bitterness, anger, and resentment.

Perhaps you are jealous, envious, or competitive to a fault. All of these emotions can lead to resentment when you don't get what you want. Bitterness, on the other hand, will affect how you behave with others. When you don't get what you want, you could become very unpleasant to deal with. You may find it hard to be friendly to someone who has done you wrong, or who has what you believe should be yours. Bitterness will leave you trapped in a cycle of negative thoughts and behavior, as well as with a heart that does not forgive. It will leave you trapped with pessimism that will adversely affect your mood, your health, and your relationships. That is why it is critical to learn to conquer it before it conquers you.

I know for myself that the root of these feelings for me came from my own sense of self-righteousness. When I felt right about a situation, the sense of being "wronged" infuriated me. I felt entitled to love and acceptance because I was "nice" had "worked hard" and did "nothing wrong." I had followed all the rules that they say you are supposed to follow, yet I still did not experience the results or acceptance that I thought I should have. This made me incredibly bitter, angry, and resentful. To be honest, the reason why I feel that I encountered these situations so frequently was because I believe that God wanted to rid me of ego and self-righteousness.

Unfortunately, this was a test that I failed miserably over and over again. Whenever I felt "wronged," I lashed out in anger. I was "nice" until you did something that was clearly "wrong." Worst, I felt justified in my behavior because I didn't "deserve" what you did, yet somehow, you "deserved" what I did back to you. How is that for circular logic!

It wasn't until I read Debrena Jackson Gandy's book, *All the Joy You Can Stand,* that it dawned on me how messed up my thinking was. The problem wasn't people's behavior; it was my expectations of how other people should behave and react. I took other people's actions and flaws as a personal attack on me, and therefore I reacted in irrational ways. I demanded unyielding loyalty from friends, or I would cut them off completely. Any act that seemed like a betrayal of trust or loyalty would be met with complete and permanent barring from my life. Looking back, I am amazed at how extreme my behavior was. Yet I know that a root cause, in addition to ego and self-righteousness, was a lack of love for myself. I didn't know how to be merciful and kind to myself, so there was no way I could show that to others. I had grown up not being shown patience, forgiveness, or genuine acceptance, so I did not know how to show that to others. I treated others the way I was treated growing up. It was the only thing I had known. Truth be told, I was even harder on myself than anyone had ever been. Thus, I didn't allow error in myself or those around me.

The old saying is true that hurting people hurt other people. Until you learn to heal and forgive yourself first and foremost, you will live behind B.A.R.s for the rest of your life. It is still a struggle, even today, to unlearn these bad behaviors, but being conscious of them is a most powerful tool in dismantling them. When people do wrong by you, first take yourself out of the equation. When you try to figure out why someone reacted the way they did, there may be many reasons that have nothing to do with you. It could be underlying hurt, a learned behavior, an honest mistake, or goodhearted ignorance. Even if it was done intentionally to hurt you, why you give them power over your emotions? What is important to understand is that a great deal of understanding is needed when dealing with people otherwise, you will become bound with emotions like anger, resentment, and bitterness.

Untangling feelings of anger, resentment, and bitterness can be very difficult. These emotions can be a stronghold over your mind and heart that make it virtually impossible to have healthy relationships with others. Just as in doing the emotional work to become your best self can be difficult, so can it be while confronting these very strong emotions. To assist in this process, I have listed some important steps you can take to overcome these destructive emotions:

1. Understand what your anger represents.

One great book about anger is *Overcoming Emotions that Destroy* by Chip Ingram and Dr. Becca Johnson. In the book, it says anger is a secondary emotion, and I have found that to be true. It says that the true underlying emotion might be something like hurt, betrayal, sadness, or embarrassment.

When you experience anger, try to be honest about the underlying emotion you are feeling. Are you just disappointed that your friend forgot your birthday when you remembered hers? Are you just frustrated that your work has not been acknowledged yet again, or are you hurt by what you perceive is a betrayal? Anger masks real emotions, and until you acknowledge what is really bothering you, anger will block healing and resolution.

Anger is also the most dangerous emotion we have as humans. It can lead to unimaginable emotional hurt as well as real physical danger. Anger can cause you to act out in the most abusive and evil way; therefore, you must learn to control it. "He that is slow to anger is better than the mighty; and he that ruleth his spirit than he that taketh a city," according to Proverbs 16:32.

Make no mistake; anger is a natural human emotion. Anger in and of itself is not bad—even Jesus experienced anger. However, anger is a problem when it occurs too frequently, lasts too long, results in inappropriate behavior, or is used in the wrong way. The wrong ways include using it to control and manipulate others, to regurgitate negative emotions, or to relieve stress. Anger can even be used to keep people at a safe distance, to avoid facing a deeper problem, or to draw attention away from the real issue. Worse, anger can be used to feel dominant and powerful.

The one good thing about anger is that it doesn't have to be your enemy. You can use it to motivate you. Many people have angered by what someone said they couldn't do or be, and they have used that anger to go out and do the very thing they were told they couldn't do. Why not add your name to that list of individuals? Emotions are not meant to be destructive. We have emotions only to satisfy or warn of a human need. When we experience anger, it is to let us know when something is missing, wrong, or uncomfortable. It can also show us when things need to be checked, fixed, or changed. Use your anger to know what needs to be changed in your life.

Martin Luther King, Jr., who is often thought of as a very peaceful person, spoke of an incident in his autobiography where anger helped propel him to his destiny. He tells the story as follows:

"When I was 14, I traveled from Atlanta to Dublin, Georgia with a dear teacher of mine, Mrs. Bradley (to) participate in an oratorical contest. We were on a bus returning to Atlanta. Along the way, some white passengers boarded the bus, and the white driver ordered us to get up and give the whites our seats. We didn't move quickly enough to suit him, so he began cursing us. I intended to stay right in that seat, but Mrs. Bradley urged me up, saying we had to obey the law. We stood up in the aisle for 90 miles to Atlanta. That night will never leave my memory. It was the angriest I have ever been in my life." He later used to anger to help usher in perhaps the greatest social change in the history of the United States.

2. Identify the source of your anger, bitterness, or resentment.

Do the work of identifying when you get angry, and how you generally express your anger. Are you even aware when you are bitter, angry, or resentful? Do you internalize it, withdraw, lash out, hold grudges, or push others away? In the book *Overcoming Emotions that Destroy*, the authors list three different anger profiles. You can basically spew it, stuff it, or leak it. Spewers are the notorious shouters and screamers who explode in a rage. They can also be manipulative since some like to scare and intimidate people to get their way.

Stuffers avoid people and situations to avoid the possibility of getting mad. Fear of conflict generally holds them back from expressing their anger.

Leakers generally become critical, sarcastic, and passive-aggressive when they get angry. They want the other person to know they are upset, but for various reasons, don't tell the person outright why. Take a moment to identify if you are primarily a spewer, stuffer, or a leaker. Awareness is the greatest tool you have for prevention.

In addition to being aware of how you express anger, you have to know the why. What things trigger your anger? Is it feeling stereotyped, disrespected, blamed, misunderstood, or something else? Problems you have had in your childhood or past relationships will help you identify what your trigger points are. Take time to identify the issues that cause you to react. Do you get angry when people question your manhood because your dad frequently called you a sissy? Do you get angry at any mention of your physical appearance because you were bullied as a child? It will be hard, but you have to unpack all of those underlying experiences and scars.

Revisit Chapter 3 if you need help in healing past emotional wounds. I think most people will be surprised to realize how much of their current relationship problems are created by unhealed emotional scars of the past. The unacknowledged baggage, assumptions, and expectations we carry with us work as a barrier to healthy relationships.

When you have identified your triggers, you will need to do either one of two things: one, work to heal an old emotional wound, or two, follow the next step listed below. For former, you can help to process old hurts through meditation exercises. For example, envision every-one that has hurt you and say, "I forgive you" to all of them. If appro-priate, you can even do this in person. Forgiveness is the penicillin for any wound that you have—it will keep it from festering and becoming infected with negativity, even if the person you are forgiving is your-self. Forgiveness releases toxic emotions and change your response to the memory. It takes the sting and helplessness out of the memory because you are controlling the dialogue. The sincerer the forgiveness, the faster the healing. The pain will never lessen without forgiveness; it will only manifest as anger and harden into resentment or bitterness. When you forgive, instead of hurt disguised as anger, you will have a lesson learned, a growing moment, or perhaps a new mission in life. I know it can be hard to go back and relive a situation that makes you feel angry or hurt, but it is necessary.

3. Change your expectations.

Perhaps, the biggest buffer to staying away from a life behind B.A.Rs is to manage your own expectations. Many times we have ex-pectations of what people should be doing for us, especially those close to us. Anytime they don't meet those expectations there is an opportunity for bitterness, anger, and resentment. First, you have to examine if your expectations are realistic. Are you expecting too much from those around you? Secondly, you have to determine what you re-ally want. You may be expecting your boyfriend to give you flowers on a regular basis, when what you really want is for him to show you in a tangible way that he cares about you. If that is the case, you may not notice all the times he fixes your car or fills your gas tank because you have a very specific idea of how his love should be shown.

To prevent bitterness, anger, and resentment, you must be honest with yourself and those around you about what you expect. First, make sure your expectations are in line with what is reasonable and achievable. Practice these conversations beforehand if you have to. Imagine a conversation with the person with whom you have a conflict. Imagine them sitting and listening without interruptions. Say everything that bothers you, how they upset you, and what they can do to fix the situation. Stay calm and honest. Now, can you see yourself having this conversation or some version of it in real life? Hopefully, the answers is yes, because people can't meet your expectations if they don't even know what they are.

The honest truth is the fewer expectations you have of others, the happier you will be. Too many expectation means you are leaving your happiness up to others to fulfill. You might look to your kids to make you feel proud, your spouse to feel loved, and your boss to feel validated. Leaving your happiness up to others is a recipe for frustration, bitterness, anger, and resentment. Instead, try to find ways to fulfill those needs on your own. Be proud of yourself, love yourself, and find work and hobbies that make you feel satisfied in your own life's purpose.

Another reason why you have to learn to meet your own needs is that even after you clearly expressed what you want and need, you still may not get it. You can't change people, nor can you control how they act or behave. So instead, develop a mechanism to accept when others say no. Otherwise, their denial of your request can morph into resentment or bitterness. Truth be told, it is also unfair to place the burden of your happiness on others. You, and you only, are in charge of your happiness. Don't give such an important task to someone else.

Another principle about expectations you need to realize is that life isn't fair. Matthew 5:45 says, "He causes his sun to rise on the evil and the good, and sends rain on the righteous and the unrighteous." Sometimes bad things happen to good people. However, allowing resentment to build up will not help the situation. You can't control life, but you can control how you respond to it. Remember, pain doesn't last forever, and it in the end, it is how we view and address a situation that will ultimately determine its effect on our lives. We can use the bad in our lives to weigh us down or to make us more determined to reach our destiny.

4. Address the emotions immediately.

When you see yourself getting angry, take steps to address it immediately. Ephesians 4:26-27 says, "In your anger do not sin; do not let the sun go down while you are still angry, and do not give the devil a foothold." Say a prayer when you start to feel angry and before you respond. Also, learn how to be a grace giver. Remember, the mercy you give is the mercy you will receive. Matthew 5:7 says, "Blessed are the merciful, for they will be shown mercy." If you feel wronged, work to forgive the other person. Forgiving is not condoning the behavior, forgetting what they did, restoring trust, agreeing to reconcile, or doing the person a favor. You are forgiving them for your own sake. Matthew 6:15 states, "But if ye forgive not men their trespasses, neither will your Father forgive your trespasses." Therefore, pray for your enemies. Confess, repent, and seek reconciliation if necessary.

When people hurt you, or you have been wronged, it is imperative that you not seek revenge. This leaves a foothold for bitterness. Revenge means your mind is stuck in that one moment, and can't move forward. It also means you are harboring intense hostility towards someone else. Most unfortunately, seeking revenge also means that you have given that person power over your emotions. You wouldn't give your enemy the keys to your car, so why are you giving them the keys to your heart?

Despite our natural inclinations, God is very clear on the subject of revenge. Romans 12:19 states, "Dear friends, never take revenge. Leave that to the righteous anger of God. For the Scriptures say, 'I will take revenge; I will pay them back,' says the Lord." As stated before, you never really know why someone did what they did. There are many times that I was enraged at someone after I was sure they had acted in malice, only later to find it was a simple misunderstanding. If I had taken revenge, I could have harmed someone who was completely innocent.

Just like you need to let people your expectations, you have to let people know when they have upset you. It's important to express to them the impact of their behavior, regardless of their intention. Express your emotions not just to get something from them, but because it is healthy for you. You can prevent a lot of unnecessary frustration and anger just by being honest about how you feel. You have to let people know what your boundaries are and what behavior you don't find acceptable. Each person has different ideas of what is acceptable behavior, and unless you are clear about what your boundaries are, people will constantly cross them. Remember that you have to let people see your needs before they can meet them.

Have conversations with those who make you angry so you can understand why they behave the way they do. Your goal is to be informed by others' behavior rather than being affected by it. This will also help stop trying to control others because you are freeing yourself from expecting them to behave a certain way. When you understand their behavior, you don't have to react to it or be controlled by it. Likewise, you can ask people to understand, hear, and acknowledge your feelings, but you do not need their validation.

Also, the way you voice your needs will affect how they are received. Instead of saying "I expect," "I want," or "I need," say "I would like," "I wish," or "I hope." Don't speak in an accusatory tone or bring up the past. Be very specific about what you are upset about, and be open to hear what the other person has to say. Again, if your wishes aren't accepted, you must make peace with that. Most likely, you will have to learn how to disengage from the person and limit your contract with them as much as possible. If someone doesn't respect your boundaries, they don't respect you, and you don't need those kinds of people in your life. Conversely, if you are not willing to tell the other party why you are angry, then let it go. It is serving no one. A reticence to tell someone what is bothering you may be a sign that you're angry over something that is petty or insignificant.

5. Learn to process your feelings of anger.

In processing anger, you can allow yourself to feel its full force, but don't let it overtake you. Acknowledge the fact that you are angry, otherwise you will be tempted to pretend that you aren't. Bottling up anger will not only be counterproductive, but it also makes room for it to manifest itself at the wrong time and in the wrong way. Don't pretend, cover up emotions, or force yourself to be happy when that's not what you are really feeling.

However, experiencing the anger and holding onto it are two different things. Letting it consume you is akin to drinking poison while hoping to make your enemies sick. You can't give other people control of your emotions. You must maintain control over yourself. The less control you have over others, the more control you need to have over yourself.

Anger is also one of the few emotions where it is not always appropriate to freely express it. Typically your upbringing will dictate what you consider a "normal" expression of anger, and your personality affects how you express it. You have to know yourself well enough to know whether voicing it will make it grow or dissipate. You have to know if you need to channel it through something like exercise, or if you need to address it directly with the person. Learning appropriate timing will be critical when dealing with anger, because as with everything, there is a time to speak and a time to be silent. Ask God for direction and understanding so that you can respond in the best way. James 1:19 says, "My dear brothers and sisters, take note of this: Everyone should be quick to listen, slow to speak and slow to become angry." Take the time to figure how the best way for *you* to manage *your* anger.

Also, take responsibility for your own feelings and behaviors as you have the final say over your mental and emotional state. Otherwise, you will see yourself as a victim instead of as someone with the power to change your situation. If you don't take responsibility for your feelings, you could become trapped into the "he or she *made* me do it" mentality. This was another powerful lesson I had to learn. No matter what people do or say to me, I am still responsible for my actions.

When I was in the military, I had a commanding officer that I did not have a great relationship with. I felt like he wanted me to kiss his butt, the way I felt he did his superiors, and that wasn't my style. During this time period, my mother had to have emergency brain surgery, and it was a very difficult time for my family. I had only so much leave I could take to be with her before I had to report back to duty. Financially, it was difficult because my mother couldn't work, and she required long-term physical therapy.

Back on the post, my stress level was high due to the situation back home, and my relationship with this officer became even more strained. One morning, my sister called asking me to wire her money for my mother's medication. That whole morning I was consumed with thoughts of my family. At the same time, this officer kept nagging me about what I considered to be insignificant things. As the tensions of the day built up, we ended up arguing, and I walked away from him.

Of course, this was not how you are supposed to respond in the military, and I was disciplined accordingly. I tried to explain to my Battalion Commander the outside strain I felt during that day, but she let me know in the end, no matter what others do, I am responsible for my actions. It was a humbling, but vital life lesson for me. No matter how much people push you, you ultimately have control over how you respond.

You have to take ownership of your part in all conflicts so that you are not a stumbling block for others. What you may not realize is that your actions might be creating anger and hurt for others. Putting your pain and feelings before others' can cause resentment and bitterness to build in those around you. Examine where you can improve your communication and relationship skills. Be the friend and spouse that you want. You can't expect everyone to adjust for you when you are not willing to do any adjusting for them. If you are unsure about what areas you need to improve on, just ask. When you find out you have offended someone, make amends for your wrongs, and ask others for forgiveness. Repent to God for the wrong that you have done, and then live free from condemnation.

6. Prevent anger, resentment, and bitterness.

The more you love yourself, the bigger buffer you have against the unkind acts people commit against you. When you are patient with yourself, you can be patient with others. When you allow yourself to make mistakes, you allow others to be human as well. You also are better at screening those in your life, so you don't attract or hang onto toxic people. Toxic people are those who keep you bitter, angry, and resentful. Self-love is medicine for the soul, because according to Proverbs 27:7, "The full soul loatheth a honeycomb; but to the hungry soul, every bitter thing is sweet." When you have self-love, you don't have to tolerate bad behavior from others as a trade-off for feeling loved.

Also, try to be less serious about yourself and life. You will experience less anger this way. If anything from someone stealing a parking spot at a grocery store to someone dirtying something of yours causes you great anger, then you have to step back and realize how insignificant these things are. Take the shouldn'ts, mustn'ts, and nevers out of your vocabulary and open your mind to new ways of doing things. Living life in a rigid box is a recipe to be in a perpetual state of anger. When you live with very rigid expectations of how things should be, you are almost guaranteeing other will let you down. Life is unpredictable, so learning to roll with the punches is one way to escape from being angry over trivial issues.

Ultimately, the reality of being a misfit is that you are more prone to bitterness, anger, and resentment because many of your expectations about how you will be received will go unmet. Your moments of rejection and ostracism can be nesting grounds for bitterness and resentment. The sad reality is that you will not be treated like everyone else, because quite frankly, you are not like everyone else. Trust me, I know that is a hard pill to swallow, but the sooner you accept that fact, the faster you can start to free up your energy and emotions for more productive ends.

It also helps if you don't take the actions of others personally. Just know that there is a place for you, and that your uniqueness will not exclude you from having love, success, or happiness. It just means the who, what, when, where, and how of those things will be different for you. Maybe you have to mourn your previous expectations—then do so and just move forward. Don't be angry, bitter, or resentful; but instead, be awesome, better, and resourceful.

Chapter Summary

Below is a recap of the steps to escape living behind bars B.A.R.s, along with the two biggest questions you need to ask yourself as you are working through these steps.

1. **Understand what your anger represents.** What underlying emotions are there? What unmet needs or issues exist?

2. **Identify the source of your anger, bitterness, or resentment.** Where do your triggers originate? Do you have unresolved emotional trauma you are dealing with?

3. **Change your expectations.** Do you know what you really expect from others? Do those around you know what those expectations are?

4. **Address the emotions immediately.** Are you seeking revenge? Have you forgiven the person?

5. **Learn to process your feelings of anger.** What is the best way for you to manage your anger? Are you taking responsibility for your part and your actions?

6. **Prevent anger, resentment, and bitterness.** Do you practice self-love? Do you have a very rigid idea of how things should be?

CHAPTER 9

Don't "Fake It 'til You Make It"

"God has given you one face, and you make yourself another."

—William Shakespeare

There is a saying that goes, "fake it to you make it" when you are working your way to success. Well, I beg to differ. This may be sound advice for normal people, but for misfits, weirdos, and introverts, it is downright dangerous. I say this because "faking it" is a slippery slope to attempting to fit in. If I am "faking it," I am not working toward being my best self. I am putting on a mask that stifles and represses me. Being authentic is more important for misfits than perhaps anyone else. So much of our destiny is tied to our unique traits and characteristics, and when we hide, alter, or mask them, it decreases our ability to fulfill our purpose.

For instance, Former First Lady Eleanor Roosevelt faced a great deal of pressure to conform to how her office was traditionally executed, yet she stayed true to who she was. By doing so, she radically changed how the role of First Lady was viewed, and she went on to become an outspoken champion for both women's rights and civil rights.

As you are moving toward the success that you want to attain, there will be times when you will want to have a tangible manifestation of your success way before it actually comes. As with most things, success always takes longer than you anticipate. Unfortunately, the desire to possess the fruit that success brings only gets stronger, and not weaker, with time. Impatience can lead us to tricky situations where we buy things we can't afford, ascend to leadership roles before we are ready, or gain notoriety before we earn respect. These situations can all lead us to a position where we are unconsciously "faking it." We could try to open a business before we know how to operate it, or live like an executive when we haven't mastered budgeting on an entry-level salary yet.

I believe social media plays a major and harmful role in this mentality. Social media sites like Facebook and Instagram are filled with people who are not even working on making it; they are just faking it. When we peruse the profiles of friends and strangers alike, we might be tempted to think they have it all. We might think that they have already made it based on what we see and read about them. These sites also provide an unnecessary temptation to play "keeping up with the Joneses."

In the end, it's another mechanism by which we feel obligated to live in this box of doing what everyone else is doing. I would caution you to limit the amount of time you spend on these sites because they can create feelings of jealousy and competition, serve as a distraction from real work, and alter what you even define as success. Luke 12:15 says, "And he said unto them, 'Take heed, and beware of covetousness: for a man's life consisteth not in the abundance of the things which he possesseth.'" In fact, several studies have found that those who are on Facebook the most also suffer from increased rates of depression. If you are using social media, use it for its intended purpose—to maintain contact with friends and family and to share your best life's moments with those you love.

As previously discussed, nothing good comes from being hasty. Pacing is important, not only to help you attain success, but also to *maintain* it. Being hasty to get to the next level will cause us to compromise on the very things that caused us to be successful in the first place—being our true selves. You have the resist the temptation to pretend like you are where you want to be. Focus instead on getting there. If you feel like you lack something important in your life, first, start by writing a list of what you think would make your life complete. Can you survive without these things right now? Most likely, the answer is yes. Learn to be content with what you have so you can actually enjoy it. Hebrews 13:5 says, "Keep your lives free from the love of money and be content with what you have, because God has said, 'Never will I leave you; never will I forsake you.'" Also remember that it is written in Galatians 6:9, "And let us not be weary in well doing: for in due season we shall reap, if we faint not." When you think about the success you desire, don't forget that God's "not yet" doesn't mean "not ever."

When you desire tangible displays of success, what you might really be looking for is some kind of buffer or security from the unpredictability of life. However, feeling secure in things is a temporary fix, not a permanent one. What you consider security could really be a wall preventing you from learning how to be strong and self-sufficient. Many times we look for shelter in things that we feel will be constant, such as money, people, or positions, but we have to realize nothing is constant. Nothing can completely shield us from the twists and turns of life. God didn't promise a carefree life; He instead promised never to leave or forsake us. Stop looking to things to shield you from rejection and pain.

Not to mention that faking it means you really haven't internalized the changes you need to make. You are just going through the motions of change. Faking it means you don't really believe what your actions are saying you do. For example, I can dress up very nicely, put on heels and makeup, and still not believe that I am beautiful. I may even attract more men, but if I suffer from low self-esteem, I still will not be able to accept that they think I am beautiful. Whereas if I truly feel beautiful, I can wear jeans and sneakers and feel like the most gorgeous woman in the room.

When you change on the inside, your actions will automatically adjust to reflect this. Using the example above, if I began to believe I was beautiful, the way I present myself and the way I carry myself would adjust accordingly. This is why it is so important for misfits not to pretend to be something they are not. The focus should always be on becoming the real deal. The desired changes will happen naturally when we do the necessary mental and emotional work.

Perhaps the only thing worse than pretending to be something that you aren't is having the disingenuous charade called out. Say, for instance, you have been pretending to have more money than you have in order to connect with those around you. At some point, you might be asked directly or indirectly to demonstrate your wealth. Now you have put yourself in the predicament of either lying more, or being exposed as a fake. Neither scenario would be beneficial to you in the end. Don't compromise your character and reputation just to satisfy a superficial desire.

Sometimes faking it can also be about hiding how we really feel. You could be pretending to feel one way when you really feel another. Whether it be to fit in, to keep peace, to gain friends, or whatever else, it is just as harmful as playing a role that is not you.

What ways do you try to hide your emotions? Do you give people the silent treatment, fake happiness, pretend to be all about business, or become passive aggressive? Ask others if you need help identifying when and how you become inauthentic. As discussed in Chapter 8, it is so important for you to tell people what you really think and feel. People can relate to you more when you are honest. They will also accept and embrace you more when they believe you are being honest with them.

Another reason why faking it is not good is because you can speak more than necessary. You may feel the need to explain why you or your life is the way it is, but in the end, you are just oversharing. Silence is golden while you are waiting for your moment. You and your life are different, and quite frankly, not everyone is going to understand that. If someone makes you feel like you have to explain why aspects of yourself or your life, I would be very cautious around that person. One, they probably feel like they are in a superior position over you if they are demanding that you explain yourself to them, and two, this person probably wouldn't get you anyway if they have to ask so many questions. Someone who cares about you may ask questions, but they will never insist that you justify yourself to them. When you feel the need to explain yourself to everyone, you are coming from a place of inferiority. The simple truth is that anyone who expects you to kowtow to them will never treat you well.

The pressure to speak could be as harmless as feeling pressure to know something you don't know. It is easy to try to pretend like you know something that you don't instead of just remaining silent or admitting the truth. Silence, however, can prevent a lot of acting out of ego. Someone might think that because they have a specific role or title, they should have the answers – including parents. Yet, so much more can be achieved by admitting when you don't have the answer. It helps others respect you more, and it helps foster team work when you work together to find shared solutions. Silence also forces you to listen to those around you. By listening, you can be in a better position to act. When you listen, you can get to the heart of an issue, show others you value what they have to say, and stop yourself from saying or doing something stupid. Proverbs 21:23 says, "Whoso keepeth his mouth and his tongue keepeth his soul from troubles."

To truly achieve greatness, there will be times that you have to shut the world out. Most times, people are not going to understand what you are trying to do. I am sure that everyone who has invented something that didn't exist prior had their ideas met with cynicism, laughter, or ridicule. Be careful who you share your dreams with; not everyone is going to understand them. When you are incubating dreams, don't let callous people cause you to abort them. Just as in pregnancy, sometimes you have to wait until your dreams have made it past a certain stage before you share your great news.

Also, please note also that if silence is golden, then paying attention is platinum. Learn to read people. As a part of learning how to interview people for visas, the State Department taught us how to read micro expressions (this is a fascinating topic to look into on your own). That training is something that I use to this day in just about every encounter I have with individuals. Don't just talk to people, but observe their reactions and facial expressions when you tell them things. What they don't say is sometimes more important than what they do say. Use and trust your intuition when dealing with people, as well. Trust yourself more than you trust the words of others. Lastly, always pray and seek God's insight into every relationship in your life.

When you have identified those who aren't good for you, end those relationships as quickly and appropriately as possible. Don't give your best to critical and judgmental people. Also, don't let others goad you into useless arguments or upset you to the point where you lose control. If you are uncomfortable sharing information, then remain silent. Some people just want to know your business, gossip behind your back, or make fun of you. Individuals should always earn your trust. You should never have blind trust in anyone other than the Lord. Proverb 4:23 says, "Above all else, guard your heart, for everything you do flows from it." Use self-love and positive thinking to override the ill intentions of others. Most importantly, don't hate these kinds of people or live behind B.A.Rs for them. They are absolutely not worth the energy.

Chapter Summary

"Faking it" will only lead you down a path where more effort is put into looking the part than being the part. It is a just another way of pretending to be something you are not. Misfits deal with the double-edged reality of having their differences be the source of both their challenges as well as their successes. Masking or attempting to deny those differences will only move us further away from our destiny.

"Faking it" will cause you to marry yourself to an idea of how you should be. The real danger to wearing masks in not just pretending to be something you are not, but thinking that something is really who you are. You will move from wearing masks to believing the masks are real. Author André Berthiaume is quoted as saying, "We all wear masks, and the time comes when we cannot remove them without removing some of our own skin." Avoid this situation altogether by being re-maining true to yourself.

There are many ways you can "fake it" in your life. You can fake who you are, how much you have, and how you feel. To combat this, there will be times in your life when silence will be golden. It is better just to keep your mouth shut than to damage your reputation by being known as someone who is untruthful. Don't succumb to the pressure to feel like you owe others an explanation about you or your life—especially those who mean you no good.

There is a Mongolian proverb that says, "Defend your name before your life," meaning that your character is the most important part of your identity. The amplified version of Proverbs 22:1 says, "A good name [earned by honorable behavior, godly wisdom, moral courage, and personal integrity] is more desirable than great riches; and favor is better than silver and gold." Don't lose your good name saying things you think people want to hear.

CHAPTER 10

Find Your Purpose and Your Passion

"Here's to the crazy ones. The misfits. The rebels. The troublemakers. The round pegs in the square holes. The ones who see things differently. They're not fond of rules. And they have no respect for the status quo. You can quote them, disagree with them, glorify or vilify them. About the only thing you can't do is ignore them. Because they change things. They push the human race forward. And while some may see them as the crazy ones, we see genius. Because the people who are crazy enough to think they can change the world, are the ones who do."

—Rob Siltanen, Creator of Apple's "Think Different" Campaign

If you have a job where you can't wait until the weekend to feel like you can start living your life, I submit to you that you are not in the right job or career for you. Life is too short to spend the majority of your day doing something you don't love; and certainly, true success will be measured not by how much you make, but whether your work fulfills you. If you find 9-to-5 cubicle work to be dreary and unfulfilling, that just might mean that you are not meant to work a conventional job.

I am a person who is always teeming with ideas, and I find it highly frustrating to be in a job where I can't share or use them. I hate stale, dry work environments that are not open to honesty or change. For me, these conditions are nonnegotiable; I simply can't work in these types of environments. If you are constantly having to face your non-negotiables at work, it's time to change how you view your work all together. We've been trained to think that work has to occur in specific places, at specific times, with specific activities, and these are just false assumptions that stop us from doing innovative, world-changing work.

One of the unique opportunities for misfits, weirdos, and intro-verts is you have the chance to redefine what a career can look like. You are an out of the box thinker, so why not bring that outlook to how you make a living? Say you like teaching, but you are not satisfied with how education is currently delivered in traditional school settings. There are opportunities for you to start a charter school, teach abroad, work in education policy, start a summer or after-school program, teach online, as well as a dozen other prospects for you to provide education in a way that is in line with your own instructional philosophies. There is literally no limit to how you can provide education to others. The same goes with many other careers.

Instead of trying to fit into the mold of what your specific career interests currently look like, make a list of the most ideal work circum-stance for you, and then look for ways to make that dream a reality. Using the example of education again, let's say you want to travel as a part of your work. You could looking into being a consultant or a trainer. If you want to work outside or with your hands, you can teach art, music, or physical education. If you want to spend more time at home with your kids, you can work from home providing virtual learning online. Stop trying to fit yourself into a specific job, but rather find a job that fits you. Dan Miller wrote a book called *48 Days to the Work You Love*, which can be useful in helping you to redefine what a career can look like.

When you envision the work you do, go even further by developing a model that hasn't even existed before. In business school, my Strategy professor said something that was a paradigm shift for me. He said most companies compete to get a slice of the pie, but smart and creative companies work to expand the pie. Meaning they don't compete for a slice of the pie in a crowded market, but they expand the pie. They accomplish this by looking for new opportunities that in the end create more opportunities for everyone.

For example, instead of just making a different brand of CD players to compete in the heavily saturated CD player market, Apple created the iPod. This generated boundless money making opportunities not only for themselves, but for others. Everyone from electronic part makers, factories, retail stores, accessory makers, and other producers in their supply chains benefited because there was now an opportunity to profit from something completely new. Even their competitors benefited because they could create copycat products that expanded their product offerings and increased their bottom line.

Why do I bring this up? Because in my opinion, you have many people competing in a crowded market of limited opportunities instead of creating new ones. There can only be so many partners at a law firm, NBA players in the national basketball league, CEOs at Fortune 500 Companies, or elected officials in a state. Therefore, instead of trying to compete with hundreds, if not thousands of other people for these limited opportunities, try to create opportunities that didn't exist before.

When you follow this approach, you not only make life better for yourself, but others can benefit as well. You can create a new product or new service that fulfills a need that was previously unmet. You can create a more efficient business model that saves times and money, and most importantly, you can employ others who were previously unemployed. You can do this all the while being authentic to yourself, and not having to fit into the predefined parameters of what success should look like. With this approach, you don't have to fit into a specific mold because you are creating a new one.

Again, there will be very strong pressure to conform and to fit in. For example, your family may be pressuring you into the field of medicine even if you struggle in science classes. If you have never had success in a specific area, it is most likely because that is not the area for you.

Conversely, doing what you are good at instead of what you love can be just as detrimental. I had a coworker who was an accountant for ten years just because she was good at math. However, her heart was always with children. It was only after ten years of successful, yet unfulfilling, work in accounting that she became a teacher. Unfortunately, she wasted a lot of time doing something she was not good at instead of what she loved. Although she wasted time, I still say it is better to pursue your dreams late rather than never. It is better to realize at some point you are on the wrong path, and take steps to fix it, than to continue down the wrong path for the rest of your life.

However, before you can find success in a specific field, you first have to know what field you want to work in long-term. If you don't know, think about your secret passion and what makes you happy. What would you do for free? What would you do if all your bills were paid? The answers to these questions will give you clues to what kind of work will be the most fulfilling to you. Alternatively, what angers you about life? What do you want to work to change? These issues can become your life mission and where you make your contribution to society. Once you figure what you really want to do, the next step is to find ways to make a living from it.

For many years, I thought I would have to be independently wealthy before I could create a non-profit that helped to provide education, but I have discovered that that is not true at all. There are many ways to start programs and non-profits without using your own money. There are federal programs and grants, as well as private foundations that support all kinds of admirable, life-changing work. The key is to do the research to find the resources and network to get you where you need to be. Subscribe to industry magazines, attend trade shows and conferences. Read books and constantly learn about different opportunities in your field.

Still, learning about a prospect is different from being ready to pursue it. You have to look before you leap. Prepare yourself sufficiently before starting any new venture. Don't think that good intentions and hard work alone is enough to be successful, for Luke 14:28 says, "Suppose one of you wants to build a tower. Won't you first sit down and estimate the cost to see if you have enough money to complete it?" Before leaving your job, improve as many situations as possible. Fix troubled relationships, acquire more skills, save money, and improve your work performance. Don't burn bridges, because you never know when you will need to cross them again. Having good references may be the difference between an open door and a closed door. Famed designer Vera Wang is quoted as saying, "Don't be afraid to take time to learn. It's good to work for other people. I worked for others for twenty years." I am not trying to imply that you should wait twenty years to pursue your dreams; I just want to emphasize that preparation is just as important as passion. Build your skill level and knowledge so that when do venture out on your own, you can achieve the highest level of success possible.

One thing you might not be expecting when you find and pursue your passion is the reality of failure. When I started my first business, a t-shirt business, I was so excited. It was a life-long dream to be an entrepreneur, and it was one of the biggest reasons why I decided to get an MBA. I spent months carefully planning all aspects of the business. I bought a plethora of t-shirt samples, made endless revisions to the graphics, and vetted many printing companies. I spared no expense to make sure the business would be successful—to the tune of about $20,000 of my own money. However, the business was an epic failure. I sold about maybe twenty-five t-shirts total over the life of that business. The experience was incredibly heartbreaking and discouraging to me. I had poured my heart into it, yet I had not been successful. It was probably the first time where I had not had success in something.

It was such a big blow to my hope, my ego, and most importantly, my pocketbook!

Despite the fact that I failed, I walked away with many new skills and many important business lessons. I could have taken that outcome to mean I was a failure, to give up on my dreams, or to live behind B.A.R.s. Instead, what I have learned through that experience is an outcome will be good or bad based on how we view it. Though it was a difficult failure, I used what I learned to build my next business faster, cheaper, and better than the first one.

When you experience failure in your own journey, don't take it as a sign that you can't be successful, that your fears are correct, or worse, take it as an assessment of your potential. Put the failure in perspective and turn it into a learning experience. Success is less a measure of someone's ability and more a measure of their determination. Some dreams will take longer to achieve than others, especially if they are innovative or counterculture. Stephen King had his first book rejected over thirty times before he was finally able to get it published!

The simple truth is that failure is a guaranteed reality of life, just like death and taxes. In fact, a majority of the world's most successful businessmen and women repeatedly failed before they ultimately found success. Henry Ford had five failed business and R.H. Macy—founder of Macy's—had seven. The founder of Sony's first invention was a rice cooker that never took off, and more than 1,000 restaurants passed on Colonel Sander's famous Kentucky Fried Chicken recipe.

This is why it is so important to pick work that you love and are passionate about because the price for true success can be high. Ultimately, it will be your love for what you do that will make you work harder, and help you to push past the many rejections and failures you might face. When you love what you are doing, it doesn't feel like work at all. I have had jobs where I looked up at 10 p.m. not realizing how much time had passed, and others where fifteen minutes felt like an eternity. The road to success is not a straight line, so find something you don't mind being in for the long haul.

Steve Jobs, founder of Apple, told Stanford graduates in a 2005 commencement speech: "Sometimes life hits you in the head with a brick. Don't lose faith. I'm convinced the only thing that kept me going was that I loved what I did. You've got to find what you love."

If you goal is just to have a lot of money, you will find success elusive. You will be doing the work you think is profitable, and not work you find enjoyable. Again, find what you love to do and learn how to make money from it. Your best and most creative ideas will come when you are working on something you are passionate about. I could be selling jewelry because that is profitable, but if I don't care about that industry, it will be hard for me to push my business to higher levels. I am not going to stay up at night thinking of new markets, new advertising ideas, or how to run my business more efficiently. I am only going to want to work for a specific period of time during the day because I don't find the work particularly rewarding. Someone who is passionate about jewelry might instead find a creative new design, seek out better and cheaper suppliers, and create a new category for customers all because they have a genuine love for what they do.

Most importantly, don't think that you need some great gift or product to have a successful venture. Use what you have, no matter how little. You can turn hobbies like cooking, sewing, and arts and crafts into global empires. Turn things you do for fun, like painting or photography, into to full-time careers. Perhaps you just like cleaning, making things pretty, or organizing things. There are boundless ways you can use those behaviors to make money. It doesn't matter what it is, just as long as you enjoy doing it. People have made literally millions on YouTube just by having others watch them play video games or play with puppets!

Even basic personality traits, such as finding fulfillment through helping others, can provide you with ample opportunities to tailor your work to your strengths. You could pursue opportunities in a number of different fields, such as healthcare, business, education, or the public sector. Furthermore, you could pursue these opportunities as an entrepreneur, employee, franchiser, consultant, trainer, or whatever role that fits you best. It could be done locally, globally, or online, and you can wear a business suit to work every day or a pair of overalls. The point is to choose whatever is best for you. The more aspects of your work that are fitted to you, the more enjoyable, fulfilling, and more successful the work will be.

If you are drawn to being your own boss, but are not interested in being a traditional entrepreneur, there are many ways that you can work in nonconventional ways. The "gig economy" is huge and is a great way to exploit and up-and-coming model of work. In this model, workers get paid for completing tasks instead of for the time they spent on the task. You can find independent contract work doing anything from driving others around, to event planning and personal training.

There are also options for freelance design work, catering, and a host of other jobs that allow you to arrange your own schedule and work as you see fit. If you are looking to be a non-traditional entrepreneur, you can look into franchising a business so you can have the support of an existing company and the blueprint of a proven business model.

Better yet, you can become an entrepreneur and run your business completely your way. The barriers to establishing a business now are almost nonexistent, and in fact, you start your own business right from the comfort of your own home via the internet. You can sell products you don't ever physically touch, as well as provide services to anyone around the world. Large platforms like Amazon, EBay, Etsy, and the like have transformed how small businesses can be run. The good news is that research has found that misfits are more likely to succeed as entrepreneurs because we tend to challenge conventional wisdom and make bold moves.

If you don't have access to traditional sources of funding, you can now use crowdfunding sites such as Kickstarter and Indiegogo. These sites have helped thousands who aren't independently rich or connected raise money to make their dreams come true. If one door closes, knock on another. Don't stop until you see the vision that is in your mind and heart.

Ultimately, the most important thing to consider when you search for the best career path is to take the restrictions off your mind of what a career can look like. Also, don't waste your energy on small endeavors. If you are taking the time to do something new, make sure it pays off appropriately in the end. Why spend all of the time and energy it takes to build something new, only for it to be the smallest, most insignificant thing you can build? That doesn't mean you can't start small; it just means that your end goal should be not to stay small. Lastly, no one is ready to receive something until they believe they can have it. Lift false assumptions off your mind of what you can do, who you are, and what you can have.

Chapter Summary

The first step to finding your path to success is not to alter your dreams to fit reality, but to alter your reality to fit your dreams. To operate in your gift, you have to create the best environment for it to manifest. Staying in a stuffy office that stifles your creativity just for money will not lead you to success. Whether you are a bookworm, a social butterfly, or a rebel, there is a work model that fits you best.

As a misfit, you may find that unconventional work models suit your gifts better. Be creative in how you make a living. You can find success working for others, for yourself, or by yourself. We live in an age where there are many jobs that allow you to work on your own schedule without setting foot outside of your home. Even if you are not ready to work for yourself, you can still find jobs that offer you flexibility in how you work. Many companies are now offering flex time and work from home opportunities. If that is the kind of freedom you want, why not pursue it? If you are unsure of exactly how to go about creating this space for yourself, the book *The 4-Hour Work Week* by Timothy Ferriss is a good resource.

Find you passion and use whatever talents you have, no matter how small. All of your quirks and oddities can be used to provide the world with something only you can supply. Explore your gifts and traits to see how to incorporate them into a career that you find fulfilling and enjoyable. Just remember that failure is an almost certain reality of working toward success. Just don't let it stop or discourage you. Use every failure as a lesson to be that much better the next time around.

CHAPTER 11

Be Thankful

"If only I'd known my differentness would be an asset, then my earlier
life would have been much easier."

—Bette Midler

When you are a misfit, weirdo, or introvert, it is easy to fall into the mental pitfall of feeling sorry for yourself, or feeling inferior. However, the best mentality to have is one of gratefulness. Why? Because your struggles have not been in vain. What we feel are just arbitrary and meaningless moments of suffering in our lives are scenarios God has placed in our paths to develop us into what He has called us to be. Author Melody Beattie believes that, "Gratitude makes sense of our past, brings peace for today, and creates a vision for tomorrow." We should be thankful not only because of our purpose, but also because there are quite a few benefits to being a misfit, weirdo, or introvert.

For instance, if you did not get into some place or circle that you thought you should be, realize that God has only spared you the time, expense, and emotion of realizing later it wasn't for you. God has only shut doors in your life because He has very specific one He wants you to walk though. Psalms 37:23 says, "The steps of a good man are ordered by the Lord." Our job is not to decide the steps, but rather to follow the steps God has given us.

Even when you struggle, God is using those experiences to mold you for the journey you have in front of you. Romans 8:28 states, "And we know that all things work together for good to them that love God, to them who are the called according to his purpose." At times, you may feel that unprotected from the trials and cruelty of life, but just know that God is using every experience in your life, both good and bad, to make your life work that much more impactful. He is using it to teach you to stand firm and to trust Him with all aspects of your life.

I remember one job that all of the other junior officers wanted—it carried a lot of status, as well as valuable work experience. I wanted to apply, but I was very scared. I felt that the job was too big for me. I felt inadequate and not good enough to be elevated to that position. Yet I felt very strongly in my spirit to apply for the job. I wrestled with these conflicting feelings for about two or three days until I submitted my application, and the moment I did so, I experienced peace. However, when I got the job, all of my fears came true. It was a very difficult job, especially for someone so introverted like myself. I could do the actual work, no problem, but I felt out of my depth with so many high-level, accomplished individuals. Worst of all, my boss was very emotionally abusive. Never in my life had I had someone make me feel so low and bad about myself. Emotionally, I was brought to the lowest point I had ever been in life. It was an incredibly painful time in my life.

After the assignment had ended, I shut the world out and fasted, prayed, and cried for about a week trying to figure out why God would lead me to a horrible experience. I never got an answer. I had to go on with life with that scar. What I didn't know then was that experience was a turning point for me. I had vowed then never to give someone power over my emotions and self-esteem ever again. I also learned not to accept abusive treatment from people. With the passing of time, that incredible hurt has morphed into incredible determination. That experience has helped me to avoid harmful people and to demand things I would have never demanded before—things such as respect, equal treatment, and pay that represents my value. In a way, I feel that that job made me a monster, but in the best way possible. I felt like my spirit has now become impenetrable to mean-spirited people, and quite frankly, I feel unstoppable.

Whatever thorn you may have to endure, remember that God has given you the grace to endure it. If you look back on your life, you will realize that your uniqueness has not stopped you from experiencing success, and in some cases, it made it even easier. Being on the outside gets you out of earshot of those who say you can't do this or that. It gets you away from the crowd of voices that say you should wear this or that, think this way or that way, or be like this or that. Misfits accomplish unique things because there is no box in their mind in which they feel the need to conform to.

There is a story about a competition of tiny frog to reach the top of a tower. Most of the other frogs didn't think they could do it, but they watched from the sidelines to observe the outcome. The higher the participating frogs hopped, the more and more frogs began to get tired and give up. The voices from the crowd saying that it was impossible also grew louder and louder. However, there was this one tiny frog that kept climbing and climbing. The higher he got, the louder the crowd yelled that it was too hard and virtually impossible. Eventually, he was the only frog left, and he made it to the top of the tower. When he made it back to the bottom, everyone asked in wonder how he had managed to make it to the top. Well, it turns out that the tiny frog was deaf! He didn't hear the crowd, so he didn't know that he "couldn't" make it to the top. Our lives as humans are just like this little frog's. If we are separated from the crowd, we also are separated from knowing whatever limitations they place on themselves and others.

These periods of isolation help us to hone in on our own voice and the voice of God as we work toward our destiny. Be thankful that they don't want to be around you. In those cases, you are spared the voices telling you what you can't do it. Even if there are detractors around, your inner voice has to be louder than all the voices around you. You have to get in tune with your intuition to help guide you to where you need to be.

When I was in the military, I met many men who were surprised at the physical things I could do. Growing up, although no one in my family told me I could do anything I wanted, I also didn't have anyone telling me I couldn't do something either. It didn't occur to me that many thought there were limits to what women could do until I joined the ROTC program in college. In my youth, I had seen plenty of very strong single mothers doing both "men's" work and "women's" work, so it never occurred to me that there was a distinction between what a woman should do and what a man should do. Therefore, I never felt fear or intimidation when it came to any of the physical aspects of being in the military. It never dawned on me that I couldn't do something. I knew that not everything would be easy, but I thought through training and practice, almost anything was possible.

If you have let the frogs get into your head about something, you are going to have to consciously change the message playing in your mind. You always have to be aware of what you are thinking and feeling, as well as what situations trigger your fears and doubts. Once you have identified those things, you must have a plan to proceed anyway. You might have to say affirmations or prayers in the beginning until your subconscious starts matching your conscious mind. However, once you have learned how to guard your heart and mind against the opinions of others, you will automatically approach situations with a mentality of possibility.

As stated before, there are numerous benefits to being different. When you are an outcast, you are almost bound to be more creative. As a misfit, you have to figure out to be successful outside of the standard way of achieving it. Misfits, for instance, learn how to lead while shy, feel confident when not viewed as attractive, and how to graduate from school when they struggle in traditional educational settings. Misfits in generally learn how to accomplish their goals without the network, support, and resources that others have.

Plus, as a misfit, you develop the mental fortitude that helps you cope with rejection, being different, and being alone. These issues aren't barriers for you because they have long been intertwined with your existence. Whenever you want to do something big or something that hasn't been done before, please understand that you will deal with those three issues in spades. Not to mention that misfits are more persistent, and quite frankly, too socially ignorant to know when to stop. These traits are so imperative for birthing trailblazing work. Normal people have not been tested so rigorously and generally can't handle the challenges of pioneering work. Abraham Lincoln struggled with shyness, and Wilma Rudolph had a physical disability that she had to work to overcome. However, those challenges helped to strengthen them for the larger calling on their lives.

Imagine a world where artists never challenged or pushed boundaries, where singers and musicians never experimented with new sounds, or fashion designers stayed with the boundaries of the same aesthetic. If everyone stayed in the lanes they were trained to be in, the world would be robbed of so much beauty and variety. You should thank God for the opportunity to bring something special and unique into the world. Be it big or small, you are here to bring something to the world that only you can give. The truer you are to yourself, the greater your gifts will manifest themselves.

You should also realize that the difficulties you face reflect God's confidence in you. One, the fact that you have not been able to fit in signals that He has something special for you to do, and two, He trusts that you have the tools and strength to bring it to life. What we must remember is that there is a gleaning process to get out what he has put in you. For example, diamonds don't exist naturally—they are created through a very arduous process. There are many stones that are easier to extract and cut, yet they are also not as valuable as the diamond. They shine like the diamond, and some even look like diamonds on the outside, yet they don't have the same value. It is because of the struggle to create the diamond that makes it so valuable.

Likewise, it is the struggles in your life that create and add to your value. These experiences are molding and shaping you into something that will shine and endure. Therefore, remember to be grateful for your life's journey, because God has chosen you to be a diamond!

Along with the benefits listed above, I have found quite a few other benefits to being different. Specifically, misfits are:

- **More insightful.** Misfits are forced to be more thoughtful and introspective because they want to understand and rationalize their experiences.

- **Can read people better.** A necessary survival trait when trying to understand those around you who are different from you.

- **More developed personalities.** Misfits can't rest on good looks, money, or any other superficial traits because they are intrinsically different from those around them.

- **Highly principled.** Misfits are more sensitive to the suffering of others and feel very strongly about what is right and wrong. They are highly empathic people who are passionate about helping others.

- **Have a greater purpose.** Every great person in the Bible stood out from those around them, whether in physical stature such as Saul and David, in wisdom and knowledge such as Solomon and Paul, or in purpose and power such as Moses and Isaiah.

In the end, instead of feeling bad about being a misfit, be thankful. Your life experiences have molded you to be something that this world had never seen. Therefore, you will be able to do things that only you can do. Focus on the purpose of why you were placed on this earth, instead of being like everyone else. Drown out the voices of the frogs that try to place limits on what you can achieve. But most of all, use the unique benefits of being a misfit to your advantage.

Chapter Summary

While it is understandable to feel that being a misfit is a disadvantage, there are many reasons to be grateful for it. Your uniqueness exists for a reason. You have to trust God to use the circumstances in your life to develop you into the person He has called you to be. Your gifts may not be apparent on the outside, but just like a diamond, you have to understand the struggles that have forged a person in order to see their real worth.

You have to know that being like everyone else is akin to being a "C" student. A grade of "C" means your work is average. Therefore, being like everyone else means you are just an average person. Think about that. If you were graded as a human being, do you want to be a "C" individual? Only those who can do what others can't get to be "As" and "Bs." As a misfit, you can never be average, so you will either be an above average person or a below average person. Being an "A" or a "B" means extra work, but it also means a greater reward. This is why is important not to be so fixated on being like everyone else. Being like everyone else only means you are average, and there is no greatness in being average.

Alternatively, being unique is kind of like being like fine china. In many homes, there are dishes you use every day, and there are others that you only use on special occasions. The times of isolation and separations are just like fine china, which is separated from the other dishes and placed by itself. Just like the china, it may appear that you will not be used, but rest assured that God is reserving you for a special purpose. He has a job for you to do that requires someone of uncommon craftsmanship, durability, and uniqueness. Just wait, your time is coming.

CHAPTER 12

R.E.L.A.X

"Excellence means when a man or woman asks of himself more than others do."

—Jose Ortega y Gasset

The final step to gaining success as a misfit, weirdo, or introvert after you have discovered and accepted who you are, worked on your emotional issues, and have become grateful, is to R.E.L.A.X. R.E.L.A.X stands for Release Every Low expectation and Act in Excellence, or written another way:

R – Release

E – Every

L – Low Expectation

A – and Act

X – in Excellence

To open your mind to different possibilities, you have to destroy your mental limits on what you perceive as possible. The world for you has to become bigger, not smaller, when you are a misfit. A small world for a misfit is debilitating, suffocating, and miserable. You can't spend your life trying to fit into a box because it will never happen. Instead, you need to see all of the different possibilities available to you. Think globally instead of locally. Remember to expand the pie, don't divide it. Constantly expose yourself to different opportunities, ideas, and people. Reading and staying current on trends in different industries will be critical for misfits because only those comfortable with ambiguity and going against the grain will be able to take advantage of groundbreaking opportunities.

Misfits are natural contenders for pioneering work because they are okay with standing out in the crowd. Most normal people will let fear of what others say and think stop them from pursuing something that seems too big or too different. When you think about what is possible in your life, remember Matthew 19:26 which says, "With man this is impossible, but with God all things are possible."

After you have released your mind from limitations on what you can have and achieve, use your intuition to decide how you will move forward. To get more in tune with your intuition, notice your body's reactions to certain environments and ideas. What thoughts and dreams keep coming back to you? A decision will feel right when it arrives unhurried. As with everything, listen for the voice of God to lead you where you need to go. Even if you have a strong desire for something, make sure that desire is coming from the right place. It could be God leading you on a specific journey, or it could be envy racing you ahead of your correct pacing.

Before you commit to a serious or lasting decision, test yourself to see if you consistently want it every day for six months. For example, you should want to marry (fill in the blank) for six months before agreeing to do it. In those six months, you should be seeking God to give you insight on what direction you should go. This decision could be anything from going back to school, moving to another location, changing your career, or opening a business. If God gives you confirmation before the six months are up, then by all means, move forward. Just make sure your relationship with God is strong enough so that you can recognize when it is actually His voice.

Once you have decided you want something, acknowledge your responsibility in making it happen. Remember, whatever is not changed is chosen. Your life is not only an accumulation of all the decisions you have made, but all of the actions you have taken. By not moving forward, you are choosing to remain in your current predicament. You can't blame God or other people for choices you have made. Your present situation will always be a reflection of your past decisions. You also have to understand that what you do is more important that what others say. For example, you could have people in your life calling you dumb, so you decide to drop out of school based on what they say. However, the reason why you don't have a degree is not because of what they said, it is because you took action and left school. Bad experiences in life won't kill you, but what they should do is show you that people can't stop you. You can only stop yourself.

Take advantage of the solitude that being unique brings, and use your alone time productively. Instead of zoning out watching TV, create something, plan something, or learn something. The celebrated author of the book *The Road Less Traveled,* M. Scott Peck, once said, "Until you value yourself, you won't value your time. Until you value your time, you will not do anything with it." Work in your own strength. Trying to be like everyone else won't help you to maximize what you bring to the table. For instance, some people are very charismatic and can motivate and rally others around a cause. However, if that is not your gift, there is no point in trying to walk in that. Perhaps your talent lies in organizing events and working behind the scenes to make sure everything goes off without a hitch. If these two individuals are working in their strengths, there is an opportunity to have a well-run event where individuals are motivated to contribute to a great cause.

Also, once you identify your strengths, don't just sit around waiting for things to happen. You have to make them happen. Everything doesn't have to be perfect in order to take advantage of opportunities. Perhaps you haven't finished your degree, but you have been presented with a business opportunity. Don't miss out because you have a false assumption about what you need to be successful. Since failure is a guaranteed fact of life, try multiple ventures in different avenues. You can do hair and makeup, provide babysitting services, or editing services on the side while you work toward your primary pursuits. You never know where those small beginnings will lead or which avenue will bring you the greatest success. Don't get tripped up into thinking your ventures have to look or be a certain way before you pursue them. You may work out of your home instead of in a storefront in the beginning. You may have to hire friends and family until you can afford a full-time staff. Just don't let the minor obstacles stop you from acting at all.

Even when you encounter major obstacles, you can still be successful. Anthony Robles, who was born without a right leg, went on to become a national wrestling champion in his senior year of college, during which year he was undefeated. Dara Torres also didn't let what others viewed as an obstacle, her age, stop her from gaining a spot on the U.S. Olympic swim team. At forty-one, she became the oldest swimmer ever to win that spot. She is also the first and only swimmer to represent the U.S. five times at the Olympics.

Still, what matters more than taking action is working in excellence. No matter if you are singing for ten people or 10,000, you should be performing at your best. It doesn't matter if you are working for a family member or the President of the United States. If someone has paid for your services, you should complete your job at the highest of your abilities. Never forget the importance of the three P's: punctual, professional, and productive. Those behaviors will do more for your success than any seminar, book, advice ever could. Proverbs 22:29 says, **"Seest thou a man diligent in his business? He shall stand before kings; he shall not stand before mean men."**

The best part of discovering what your goals are and working toward them is realizing that when you are on the right path for your life, doors will open. When I decided to go to an out of state, private college, I did not have the means or the guidance to forge that path. Yet I felt very passionately about going to this one school. In fact, it was the only college I applied to until my guidance counselor admonished me about me putting such limitations on myself. I applied to one more school, but I had my heart set on my dream school. Thankfully, God blessed me to attend that university. In the end, if that path is meant for you, God will make a way for you to walk down it.

At this stage of my journey as a misfit, I am at the place where I have not only accepted my uniqueness, but I also embrace it. I love the solitude that being a misfit provides. There is a real freedom you get from not truly belonging to any one place or group. I have quietly (and not so quietly) done whatever I wanted to do because I am not bound to some group's rules of how to live. Because I have a very strong sense of self and purpose, I don't allow people to define who I am anymore.

Learning how to be successful as a misfit, weirdo, or introvert is moving away from involuntary ignorance to intentional control of your thoughts, emotions, and actions. Most importantly, it is not only accepting that you are different, but embracing all the unique things about yourself. Put an end to the desire to fit in and be like everyone else. If that is what God meant for your life, that is how your life would be. Stand boldly, armed with the knowledge that you were uniquely designed to be exactly as you are. Famous country singer Shania Twain is quoted as saying, "I find that the very things that I get criticized for, which is usually being different and just doing my own thing and just being original, is the very thing that's making me successful." If we keep that mentality in mind, we can understand that our differences don't keep up from success—they actually create it.

With the help of God, and hopefully this book, I am confident you will reach your highest form of acceptance, freedom, and success.

Chapter Summary

The journey of self-discovery is a long one, so when you come to a place where you are ready to find your own path, it is important not to place limits on what that path can look like. God is planning something for your life that is bigger than what you can even imagine. 1 Corinthians 2:9 states that, **"But as it is written, eye hath not seen, nor ear heard, neither have entered into the heart of man, the things which God hath prepared for them that love him."**

Still, just dreaming big is not enough. You first have to confirm that your dreams are in alignment with what God has for your life, and once you do that, you have to act. You can't waste your time sitting around expecting things to happen. Just believing you can be successful is not enough. James 2:17 says, "In the same way, faith by itself, if it is not accompanied by action, is dead." And when you do act, make sure that you act in excellence. It is only with by acting in excellence that you achieve the full breadth the success that is meant for you. Your success is tied to what makes you unique, so make sure you are the best you possible.

At the end of the day, anything that causes you to change who you are just to fit in is not good for you. Many people feel pressure to conform because they feel naked without the masks that everyone else wears. Well, the question to ask yourself is: What happens if people see the real you? What is wrong with the naked version of you?

This is why it is important to work to be the best you possible. When you live without masks, you are forced to make sure what is exposed is actually worth showing. It's kind of like wearing sandals. If my feet are hidden, I probably don't care much about how they look, but if they are visible, I am going to take care that I present them the best way possible. Well, live life with the real you exposed—that way, you will take care to make sure that you are presenting the best you possible.

www.ingramcontent.com/pod-product-compliance
Lightning Source LLC
Chambersburg PA
CBHW031515040426
42445CB00009B/235